Facts about Germany

CONTENTS

FOREWORD

What characterises politics, business, society, academia, and culture in Germany? "Facts about Germany" invites readers to get to know the modern and cosmopolitan country. The handbook offers exhaustive basic information and numerous points of orientation – all specially designed with international readers in mind. In nine chapters, "Facts" conveys a basic understanding of German society and shows which models and solutions are being discussed in a time of social and political change. The completely revised new edition focusses in particular on contemporary issues – historical and institutional references take a backseat. In order to make the texts as useful as possible, they include up-to-date information and statistics.

The continued development of "Facts about Germany" includes giving it a broad digital presence, exploring in more depth online the topics outlined in the print edition. The new "Facts about Germany" community, which we cordially invite you to join, is at the same time intended to promote dialogue and serve as a platform for the exchange of ideas. ∎

Get to know Germany – with the cross-media "Facts about Germany"

FACTS FAMILY

Insight: Informative overviews spotlight current developments in the topic explored in each chapter.

HANDBOOK

In its nine chapters the new edition of the handbook "Facts about Germany" offers a whole host of different angles on present-day Germany. Each of the chapters is structured in such a way that an "Insight" first provides the most important basic information on the topic in question by way of introduction. Subsequently, the various aspects of the topic are explored in depth. Moreover, each chapter contains numerous references to further sources of information as well as cross-media services.

Topic: Fact-based texts offer an in-depth and expanded consideration of the key aspects.

→ **Information in 19 languages**
→ **Nine chapters**
→ **Various information levels**
→ **Tips for further information**
→ **Key players in each topic**
→ **Print-to-Web links via augmented reality applications**

FACTS FOR YOUNG ADULTS

How can young people get to know Germany? What brings the country to life for them; what should future high potentials know? The new 76-page "Facts" handbook for young people provides informative insights in nine languages – also online.
facts-about-germany.de

Panorama: Extensive info graphics complement the chapters, adding an exciting visual component.

facts-about-germany.de:
Modern design meets concentrated information.

DIGITAL

The completely redeveloped Website **facts-about-germany.de** is the heart of the extensive multimedia digital offerings. What is more, the responsive design enables optimum use on mobile end devices. The "Facts" range also includes e-paper editions and e-reader services. The information on facts-about-germany.de is dynamically structured and regularly supplemented and updated, on all channels.

→ Information in 19 languages
→ Videos and interactive graphics
→ Additional chapter "German History"
→ Extensive background information
→ Regular supplementation on important
   political, social, and cultural issues

VIDEO ▢ AR APP

Additional digital material
1. Download the free app "AR Kiosk" from your app store onto your mobile device. "AR Kiosk" is available from iTunes and Google Play.

2. Start the app and hold your smartphone or tablet over the image with the icon Video & AR app (pages 23, 39, 59, 79, 95, 115, 135, 155). Additional digital information is available via these pages.

3. As soon as the app has recognised the image, the bonus material will automatically open.

WELCOME TO THE COMMUNITY
Those wanting to find out more about Germany and stay up to date can join the new "Facts about Germany" community. Amongst other things, members of the network exclusively receive the "Facts Newsletter". Subscribe via the Website.

AT A GLANCE

Federal Republic • Crests & Symbols • Demographics •
Geography & Climate • Parliament & Parties • Political System •
Federal Government • Famous Germans

FEDERAL REPUBLIC

Germany is a federation. The federation and the 16 Länder (states) each have areas of responsibility of their own. Responsibility for internal security, schools, universities, culture, and municipal administration lies with the states. The administrative authorities of the states enforce not only their own laws, but also those of the federation. Through their representatives in the Bundesrat the governments of the states are directly involved in the federation's legislation.

Federalism in Germany is more than just a system of federal states; it represents the country's decentral cultural and economic structure and is deeply rooted in tradition. Over and above their political function, the states are also a reflection of pronounced regional identities. The strong position of the states was established in the Basic Law in 1949; on reunification in 1990, five new states were founded: Brandenburg, Mecklenburg-West Pomerania, Saxony, Saxony-Anhalt, and Thuringia. With 17.6 million inhabitants, North Rhine-Westphalia is the most populous state, while its 70,550 square kilometres make Bavaria the largest in terms of surface area; with 3,838 inhabitants per square kilometre Berlin, the capital, is the most densely populated. There is one peculiarity: the three city states. Their territory is restricted in each case to a major city, namely Berlin, Bremen and Hamburg. With 419 square kilometres and 657,000 inhabitants, Bremen is the smallest state. Economically speaking, Baden-Wurttemberg is one of the strongest regions in Europe. After the Second World War, Saarland was a partly sovereign state and a French protectorate, and was only integrated in the former territory of the Federal Republic as the tenth state on 1 January 1957. ∎

The 16 federal states

SCHLESWIG-HOLSTEIN

Kiel

MECKLENBURG-WEST POMERANIA

Schwerin

HAMBURG

BREMEN

LOWER SAXONY

BRANDENBURG

BERLIN

Hannover

Magdeburg

Potsdam

NORTH RHINE-WESTPHALIA

SAXONY-ANHALT

Düsseldorf

Erfurt

Dresden

HESSEN

THURINGIA

SAXONY

Wiesbaden

RHINELAND-PALATINATE

Mainz

SAARLAND

Saarbrücken

Stuttgart

BAVARIA

BADEN-WÜRTTEMBERG

Munich

● State capital

Federal Eagle

The Federal Eagle is the German state symbol that is the richest in tradition. The Federal President, the Bundesrat, the Federal Constitutional Court, and the Bundestag use differently styled eagles. The eagles that appear on coins and the national strip of German sports associations also differ in terms of design.

Basic Law

Passed in 1949 in Bonn, the Basic Law was initially intended to be provisional. After reunification in 1990 the version was then adopted as the permanent constitution. The 146 Articles of the Basic Law supersede all other German legal norms and define the basic systems and values of the state.

Flag

The Basic Law states that the colours of the federal flag shall be black, red, and gold. In 1949, this followed on from the flag of the first German republic of 1919. The Nazis had abolished the latter and replaced it with the swastika.

National Holiday

As the Day of German Unity, in the Unification Treaty of 1990 3 October was declared a national holiday in Germany. The Day of German Unity is the only national holiday to be determined by federal law.

Currency

The euro has been the legal tender in Germany since 1 January 2002. It replaced the deutschmark, which had been in use since 1948. The European Central Bank (ECB) is headquartered in the German financial centre Frankfurt am Main.

Domain

The domain ".de" is the most widespread country-specific domain in Germany, and the most popular worldwide. Using the international dialling code +49, 99.9 percent of households can be reached via landline or mobile telephone.

National Anthem

The German national anthem consists only
of the third stanza of the Deutschlandlied by August
Heinrich Hoffmann von Fallersleben (1841). The
melody was written by Joseph Haydn in 1796-97.

Ei – nig – keit und Recht und Frei – heit
Da – nach lasst uns al – le stre – ben

für das deut – sche Va – ter – land!
brü – der – lich mit Herz und Hand!

Ei – nig – keit und Recht und Frei – heit

sind des Glü – ckes Un – ter – pfand.

Blüh im Glan – ze die – ses Glü – ckes,

blü – he, deut – sches Va – ter – land!

DEMOGRAPHICS

With regard to demographic developments there are three clear trends in Germany: a low birth rate, rising life expectancy, and an aging society. With 1.357 million new born babies, Germany registered its highest birth rate in 1964, since when the country has been at a low as far as births are concerned (in 2014 there were 715,000 new babies born). Since 1975 the average number of births, allowing for slight fluctuations, has been about 1.3 children per woman. As such, for 35 years the generation of children has been about a third smaller than that of its parents – nowadays there are twice as many 50-year olds as there are newborn babies. At the same time life expectancy is rising. For men it is on average 77 years, for women 82 years.

The demographic changes and the serious impact this has on economic development and the welfare systems is being cushioned by immigration. A total of 20.3 percent of the people living in Germany (16.4 million) have a migration background: 9.2 million of them have a German passport, 7.2 million are foreigners. Members of four national minorities are recognized as having long-established roots and enjoy special protection and support: the Danish minority (50,000) and the Friesian ethnic group (60,000) in north Germany, the Lusatian Sorbs (60,000) along the German-Polish border, and the German Sinti and Roma (70,000). ∎

LIFE EXPECTANCY
82 years / 77 years
Women   Men

IMMIGRANTS IN 2013
1,226,000

EMIGRANTS IN 2013
789,000

HOUSEHOLDS
40.2 m

POPULATION

81.2 m

GENDER DISTRIBUTION

41.4 m

Women

39.8 m

Men

AGE STRUCTURE

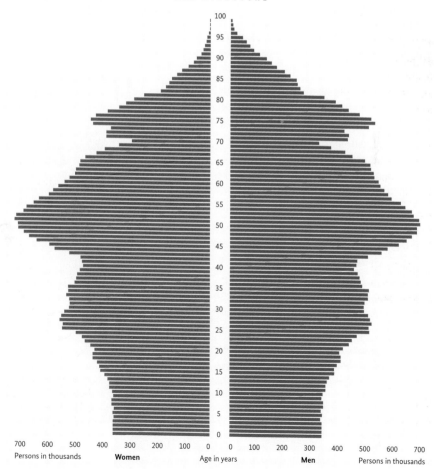

Source: Federal Statistical Office, 2014

700   600   500   400   300   200   100   0   0   100   200   300   400   500   600   700

Persons in thousands   Women   Age in years   Men   Persons in thousands

GEOGRAPHY & CLIMATE

Germany lies at the heart of Europe. It shares its borders with nine other nations. No other European country has more neighbours. In the north, Germany has access to the North and Baltic Seas. In the south it borders on the Alps. At 2,962 metres the Zugspitze in Bavaria is its highest peak. At 3.54 metres below sea level the lowest point on land is near Neuendorf-Sachsenbande in Schleswig-Holstein. Measuring 357,340 square kilometres, Germany is the fourth largest country in the European Union (EU) after France, Spain, and Sweden. Forests cover almost a third of its total surface area. Lakes, rivers, and other inland waters account for more than two percent. The Rhine is the longest river. In the southwest it marks the border between Germany and France, further north Bonn, Cologne, and Düsseldorf all lie on its banks. The Elbe, the second longest river, links Dresden, Magdeburg, and Hamburg and flows into the North Sea.

Germany enjoys a moderate climate. In July, the mean maximum temperature is 21.8 degrees Celsius, the minimum 12.3 degrees. In January, the mean maximum is 2.1 degrees, the minimum −2.8 degrees. The highest temperature since records began was recorded on 5 July 2015 in Kitzingen am Main, namely 40.3 degrees Celsius. ∎

LOCATION
Central Europe

SURFACE AREA
357,340 km^2

CAPITAL
Berlin
891.70 km^2

HOURS OF SUN
1,670

RAIN
729 l/m²

COASTLINE
1,200 km

LONGEST RIVER
Rhine
865 km in Germany

FORESTED AREA
114,191 km²

HIGHEST MOUNTAIN
Zugspitze
2,962 m

PARLIAMENT & PARTIES

The German Bundestag is elected every four years by free, secret, and direct ballot by citizens aged 18 and over who are eligible to vote. The Bundestag is the German parliament. Half of the at least 598 seats in the Bundestag are allocated through the election of candidates put up by the parties on state lists (second votes), the other half through the election of persons in 299 constituencies (first votes). The German electoral system makes it difficult for any one party to form a government on its own – meaning that a coalition tends to be the rule. In order to prevent complications in the formation of majorities by the presence of small and very small parties, a threshold, known as "the five percent hurdle" excludes parties that poll less than that being represented in the Bundestag. Five parties are currently represented in the Bundestag: CDU, CSU, SPD, The Left party, and Alliance 90/The Greens. Ever since the first election to the Bundestag in 1949, CDU and its sister party CSU, which only stands in Bavaria, have formed a single parliamentary party. In the 2013 election to the Bundestag, the Free Democratic Party (FDP) failed to clear the five percent hurdle and is thus not represented in the Bundestag for the first time since 1949. The current Federal Government is made up of a coalition of CDU/CSU and SPD, with Dr. Angela Merkel (CDU) as the Federal Chancellor, Sigmar Gabriel (SPD) as Deputy Chancellor and Dr. Frank-Walter Steinmeier (SPD) as Federal Foreign Minister. The Left party and the Greens form the parliamentary opposition. ∎

Parties

CDU

**Christian Democratic Union
of Germany (CDU)**
457,488 members
2013 election result: 34.1 percent

**Social Democratic Party
of Germany (SPD)**
459,902 members
2013 election result: 25.7 percent

DIE LiNKE.

The Left party
60,547 members
2013 election result: 8.6 percent

Alliance 90 / The Greens
60,329 members
2013 election result: 8.4 percent

Christian Social Union (CSU)
146,536 members
2013 election result: 7.4 percent

Bundestag

The Bundestag has at least 598 members.
In addition, there tend to be what are known
as "overhang and equalising" seats. The 18th
Bundestag as elected in 2013 has 630 members.

630 seats

CSU
56 seats

The Left party
64 seats

CDU
254 seats

SPD
193 seats

Greens
63 seats

Bundesrat

The Bundesrat is one of five permanent constitutional
bodies. It represents the Länder, the federal states.
The Bundesrat is made up of 69 representatives
of the state governments. Each state has at least three,
the most populous state up to six votes.

Baden-Wurttemberg **6**

Bavaria **6**

Berlin **4**

Brandenburg **4**

Bremen **3**

Hamburg **3**

Hessen **5**

Mecklenburg-West Pomerania **3**

4 Thuringia

4 Schleswig-Holstein

4 Saxony-Anhalt

4 Saxony

3 Saarland

4 Rhineland-Palatinate

6 North Rhine-Westphalia

6 Lower Saxony

POLITICAL SYSTEM

In terms of protocol, the Federal President is Germany's most senior representative. The President of the Bundestag is, in terms of protocol, the second most senior. The proxy for the Federal President is the President of the Bundesrat – an office held on an annual basis by the premier of the one of the federal states. The office with the greatest political power is that of the Federal Chancellor. The President of the Federal Constitutional Court is likewise one of the country's high representatives. ▪

The people

elect

All German citizens aged 18 and over are eligible to vote. They elect MPs in a general, direct, free, and equal election by secret ballot.

elect

Joachim Gauck, b. 1940, independent, Federal President since March 2012

Dr. Angela Merkel, b. 1954, CDU, Federal Chancellor since November 2005

State parliaments

As a rule the legislature of the state parliaments is five years. The state constitutions regulate their powers and how they are organised.

send delegates to

elect

State governments

Dr. Norbert Lammert, b. 1948, CDU, Bundestag President since 2005

Dr. Andreas Vosskuhle, b. 1963, President of the Federal Constitutional Court

The state governments are elected in each case by the state parliaments in a secret vote, and can also be brought down by them.

send delegates to

The Bundestag

elects →

The parliament is elected for four years and has 598 members. In addition there are so-called overhang and equalising seats. The Bundestag is responsible for legislation and monitoring government.

The Federal Chancellor

proposes →

The Chancellor is elected by the Bundestag in a secret vote. The Chancellor determines policy guidelines and is head of the Cabinet.

The Federal Government

The government comprises the Federal Chancellor and the federal ministers. Each minister runs his or her ministry independently.

elects

sends delegates to

The Federal Assembly

The Federal Assembly convenes solely for the purpose of electing the Federal President, whom it elects in a secret vote for a five-year term of office.

elects

appoints

appoints

The Federal President

The head of state's duties are primarily of a representative nature and he represents the Federal Republic in international matters. He appoints the Chancellor and the federal ministers and issues laws.

The Bundesrat

The chamber of states is made up of 69 members delegated by the state governments. In many fields laws require the approval of the Bundesrat.

elects

elects

elects

Federal Constitutional Court

The Court has 16 judges. Half of them are elected with a two thirds majority by the Bundestag and Bundesrat.

FEDERAL GOVERNMENT

The Federal Chancellor and the federal ministers form the Federal Government, the cabinet. Alongside the Chancellor's power to set policy guidelines, within these general parameters ministers on principle run their ministries independently; the collective principle also applies, whereby the Federal Government settles disputes by majority decision. The federal cabinet consists of 14 ministers and the Head of the Federal Chancellery. The federal ministries are the highest federal authorities for the relevant departments. The Basic Law assigns the Chancellor a special role: "The Federal Chancellor shall determine and be responsible for the general guidelines of policy". The Federal Chancellery and the federal ministries employ around 18,000 staff members. The Federal Foreign Office and the Federal Ministry of Defence are among the ministries with large payrolls. Eight ministries are based in Berlin, six in the Federal City of Bonn. All the ministries maintain offices in both cities. ∎

Federal Ministries

Federal Ministry for Economic Affairs
and Energy
→ bmwi.de

Federal Foreign Office
→ auswaertiges-amt.de

Federal Ministry of the Interior
→ bmi.bund.de

Federal Ministry of Justice and
Consumer Protection
→ bmjv.de

Federal Ministry of Finance
→ bundesfinanzministerium.de

Federal Ministry of Labour and Social Affairs
→ bmas.de

Federal Ministry of Food and Agriculture
→ bmel.de

Federal Ministry of Defence
→ bmvg.de

Federal Ministry of Family Affairs,
Senior Citizens, Women and Youth
→ bmfsfj.de

Federal Ministry of Health
→ bmg.bund.de

Federal Ministry of Transport
and Digital Infrastructure
→ bmvi.de

Federal Ministry for the Environment,
Nature Conservation, Building and
Nuclear Safety
→ bmub.bund.de

Federal Ministry of Education and Research
→ bmbf.de

Federal Ministry for Economic
Cooperation and Development
→ bmz.de

Federal Presidents & Federal Chancellors

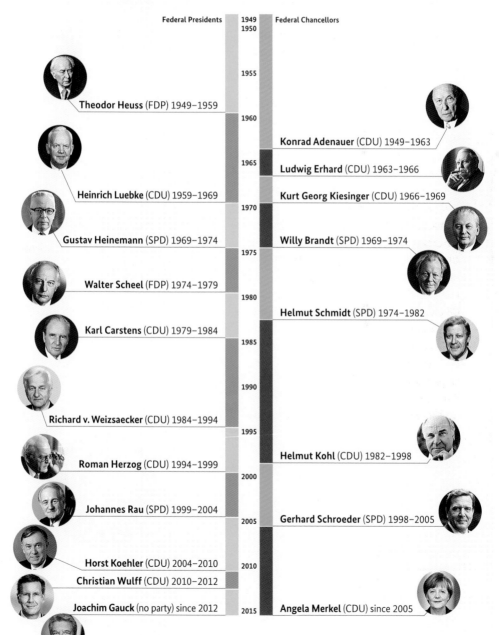

Federal Presidents

1949
1950

1955

Theodor Heuss (FDP) 1949–1959

1960

Heinrich Luebke (CDU) 1959–1969

Gustav Heinemann (SPD) 1969–1974

1965

1970

1975

Walter Scheel (FDP) 1974–1979

1980

Karl Carstens (CDU) 1979–1984

1985

1990

Richard v. Weizsaecker (CDU) 1984–1994

1995

Roman Herzog (CDU) 1994–1999

2000

Johannes Rau (SPD) 1999–2004

2005

Horst Koehler (CDU) 2004–2010

Christian Wulff (CDU) 2010–2012

2010

Joachim Gauck (no party) since 2012

2015

Federal Chancellors

Konrad Adenauer (CDU) 1949–1963

Ludwig Erhard (CDU) 1963–1966

Kurt Georg Kiesinger (CDU) 1966–1969

Willy Brandt (SPD) 1969–1974

Helmut Schmidt (SPD) 1974–1982

Helmut Kohl (CDU) 1982–1998

Gerhard Schroeder (SPD) 1998–2005

Angela Merkel (CDU) since 2005

FAMOUS GERMANS

Celebrated classics, courageous visionaries, astute thinkers: Germany's history is rich in people who achieved extraordinary things. Many of them are famous far beyond the country's borders. The Goethe-Institut has been indirectly spreading the name of the most well-known of all Germans, Johann Wolfgang von Goethe, throughout the world since 1951. In Paris, the Maison Heinrich Heine at Cité Internationale Universitaire de Paris (CIUP) keeps alive the memory of the gifted literary figure, who had a chronic soul-searching relationship with his home country. Wagner fans from all over the world congregate every year at the Bayreuth Festival to pay homage to "Der Ring des Nibelungen". Names such as Humboldt and Einstein, Röntgen and Planck, Benz and Otto established Germany's reputation as a country of researchers and engineers.

In earlier days, women faced difficulties leading similarly high-profile lives. Yet there are nonetheless many famous women, such as Clara Schumann, Maria Sybilla Merian, Paula Modersohn-Becker, Rosa Luxemburg, Anna Seghers, and the great choreograph Pina Bausch. They are to this day regarded as role models for a modern society which enables men and women alike to participate and enjoy equal opportunities – even though this still requires a concerted effort. ∎

Johann Wolfgang von Goethe

Poet, playwright, scholar: Johann Wolfgang von Goethe (1749–1832) is regarded as an all-round genius and the classic in German literature.

Friedrich von Schiller

A fighter for freedom: Friedrich von Schiller (1759–1805) is regarded as one of the world's great playwrights ("The Robbers", "Mary Stuart", "Don Carlos") and as an important essayist.

Johann Sebastian Bach

Virtuoso of Baroque church music: Johann Sebastian Bach (1685–1750) perfected the strict "art of the fugue" and composed more than 200 cantatas and oratorios.

Marlene Dietrich

The film diva: Marlene Dietrich (1901–1992) was
one of only a few German actresses to become an icon
("The Blue Angel"). Born in Berlin, she took
US citizenship in 1939.

Ludwig van Beethoven

Pioneer of Romanticism: Ludwig van Beethoven
(1770–1827), focussing clearly on form, brought a
completely new measure of personal expression and
sensitivity to bear in music ("9th Symphony").

Thomas Mann

A master of the novel and novella:
Thomas Mann (1875–1955) is one of the most
important authors of 20th-century world literature.
In 1929 he was awarded the Nobel Prize in
Literature for his family saga "Buddenbrooks".

Albrecht Dürer

German Renaissance artist:
Albrecht Dürer (1471–1528) from Nuremberg is
one of the most important and versatile figures in the
history of art. He revolutionised woodcarving and
copperplate engraving techniques.

Wilhelm Conrad Röntgen

Discoverer of X-rays: Wilhelm Conrad Röntgen
(1845–1923) discovered X-rays in 1895 in Würzburg.
In 1901 he was awarded the Nobel Prize in Physics.
Since then more than 80 leading German scientists
have received a Nobel Prize.

Willy Brandt

Politician and cosmopolitan: Willy Brandt (1913–1992)
as Federal Chancellor from 1969–1974 initiated a
policy of detente; like no other he embodied the
democratic and social changes of the time – in 1971 he
received the Nobel Peace Prize.

THE STATE & POLITICS

Successful Reforms • Federal State • Active Politics •
Broad Participation • Vibrant Culture of Remembrance

INSIGHT
SUCCESSFUL REFORMS

Today, 25 years after reunification, Germany is a value-based, democratic, economically successful, and cosmopolitan country. The political landscape is diverse; the democratic parties compete against one another – but they also have mutual respect for one another and form coalitions at various political levels. Since the elections for the 18th German Bundestag in 2013, Germany has been governed by a Grand Coalition of CDU/CSU and SPD, an alliance of the two major forces in the German party system. Of the 630 Members of Parliament, the coalition partners account for 503 seats (CDU/CSU 310, SPD 193). The opposition has 127 seats, with The Left party holding 64 and Alliance 90/The Greens 63 of them, making it the smallest parliamentary opposition for over 40 years. Federal Chancellor Dr. Angela Merkel (CDU), the first female head of a German government, has been in power since 2005 and is now in her third term of office.

She is the first woman in the history of the Federal Republic of Germany to hold this office. Merkel grew up in former East Germany, where she gained a doctorate in Physics. In rankings by Forbes Magazine in 2014 and 2015 she took first place in the list of the world's most powerful women. Deputy Chancellor Sigmar Gabriel (Federal Minister for Economic Affairs and Energy) and Dr. Frank-Walter Steinmeier (Federal Foreign Minister) are important representatives of the SPD in the Cabinet. The Cabinet is made up of 14 ministers and the Head of the Federal Chancellery. The Coalition Agreement entitled "Shaping Germany's Future" serves as the basis of the government parties' joint work for the current legislature until 2017.

In 2016, the German economy will enter its seventh year of consecutive growth, employment is at a record high, and government revenue ▶

VIDEO 📹 **AR APP**

The State & Politics: the video on the
topic → **tued.net/en/vid1**

The Reichstag Building in Berlin has been the seat of the German Bundestag since 1999. Sir Norman Foster designed the glass dome

▶ and national insurance contributions have risen. New debt assumed by central government has been reduced to zero. The Energy Reform is being driven forward – renewable energies are on the way to becoming the decisive technology for generating electricity. Furthermore, the reform of the social welfare systems in the early 2000s, a policy programme that went by the name of Agenda 2010, ensured that Germany weathered the financial crises since 2008 better than other countries in the Eurozone.

Together, the people in Germany have made the gradual fusion of east and west Germany, a major issue since 1990, into a success story. The "Solidarity Pact II", for which 156.5 billion euros are set aside, will remain in force until 2019. All tax-paying citizens in the east and west continue to play a joint role in the "Aufbau Ost" project to redevelop the east through the "solidarity surcharge", a supplementary contribution which today stands at 5.5 percent of personal income tax.

That said, new tasks await. As in other industrialised countries, demographic change and the associated ageing and contracting population are regarded as a challenge. Not least of all for this reason Germany intends to simplify immigration and make it easier for new citizens to become integrated.   ∎

→ **INTERNET**

The German Bundestag
Elections, Members of Parliament, parliamentary groups
→ bundestag.de

The Bundesrat
Composition, duties, sessions
→ bundesrat.de

The Federal President
State visits, appointments, duties
→ bundespraesident.de

Chaired by Federal Chancellor Merkel, the federal cabinet meets every Wednesday at 9.30 a.m. in the Federal Chancellery

PLAYERS & ORGANISATIONS

Political parties

Germany is a party-based democracy. Five parties are represented in the 18th German Bundestag – CDU, CSU, SPD, The Left party and Alliance 90/The Greens. There are also around 25 small parties, whose influence is limited on account of the five percent hurdle. Some of them are represented, however, in various federal state parliaments. The Social Democratic Party of Germany (SPD) is the party with the most members (461,000). The Christian Democratic Union (CDU) has around 459,000 members, its sister party the Christian Social Union (CSU) in Bavaria 147,000 (2014).

→ **bundeswahlleiter.de**

Trade unions

The German Trade Union Confederation (DGB) embraces eight individual trade unions and has 6.1 million members. With 2.3 million members IG Metall, the metal workers' union, which among other things represents workers in the automotive sector, is the single largest union. The trade unions' ideas have weight and influence in political debates.

→ **dgb.de**

Industrial federations

As industry's umbrella organisation, the Federation of German Industries (BDI) unites 36 sector federations and speaks on behalf of around 100,000 companies.

→ **bdi.de**

Social movements

Since the 1970s many people in Germany have been actively involved in environmental groups, citizens' movements, and non-government organisations. With half a million members, Friends of the Earth Germany (BUND) is the largest environmental association.

→ **bund.net**

Public opinion research

Numerous opinion research institutes regularly conduct research into the political climate in Germany. Institutes such as infratest dimap, Allensbach, Forsa, Emnid and Forschungsgruppe Wahlen have a particularly strong presence in the run-up to elections, but also with up-to-date weekly barometers that indicate the general mood.

➕ DIGITAL PLUS

More information about all the topics in the chapter – annotated link lists, articles, documents; plus more in-depth information about terms such as Bundesrat, Federal Government, federal state, Bundestag, Federal Constitutional Court, Basic Law, electoral system.

→ **tued.net/en/dig1**

FEDERAL STATE

Germany is a parliamentary and federal democracy. The German Bundestag, the constitutional body most present in the public eye, is directly elected by citizens eligible to vote every four years. The most important tasks of the Bundestag are legislation and to oversee the government's work. The Bundestag elects the Federal Chancellor for the legislative period by secret ballot. Within the Federal Government the Chancellor has the authority to lay down guidelines, in other words determines binding broad policy lines. The Federal Chancellor appoints the federal ministers, and from among them a Deputy Chancellor. In actual fact, however, it is the parties that make up the government that decide which persons will head the ministries they were allocated in the coalition negotiations. If a coalition collapses, the Chancellor can also fall prior to the end of the electoral term, as the Federal Government has the right to vote the head of government out of office at any time. In such cases parliament must, however, name a successor at the same time in what is known as a "constructive vote of no confidence". This means that there can be no period of time without an elected government in office.

Coalition governments are
the rule in Germany

The system of personalised proportional representation is decisive with regard to the character of the parliament. This way, smaller parties are also represented in the Bundestag in proportion to their election results. For this reason, with one exception, the Federal Government has always been formed through an alliance of several parties that had competed against each other in the election; since the first Bundestag election in 1949 there have been 23 coalition governments. To avoid fragmentation in parliament and make forming a government easier, parties must poll at least five per cent of the votes cast (or three direct mandates) in order to be represented in the Bundestag (this rule is known as the five percent hurdle).

☰ LIST

- Largest federal state: **North Rhine-Westphalia (17.6 million inhabitants)**

- Highest individual federal ministry budget: **Labour and Social Affairs (122 billion euros)**

- Largest Bundestag committee: **Economic Affairs and Energy (46 members)**

- Highest turnout: **1972 election to the Bundestag (91.1 percent)**

- Largest parl. party: **CDU/CSU (310 MPs)**

On the roof of the Reichstag in Berlin: around 8,000 people visit the parliamentary building every day

Germany's federal character is revealed in the large level of independence the 16 federal states enjoy, in particular with regard to the police, disaster control, the law, and culture. For historical reasons the cities of Berlin, Hamburg, and Bremen are also federal states. The close links between the federal states and central government is unique, resulting in the state governments having numerous opportunities to play an active role in central government policy. This occurs primarily through the Bundesrat, the upper house, which is made up of members of the federal state governments and is likewise in Berlin. Densely populated federal states have greater representation in the Bundesrat than smaller ones. By being coalition partners in federal state governments, parties that at federal level are in opposition, or not even represented in the Bundestag, can thus potentially exert an influence on politics at federal level, as numerous federal acts and ▶

decrees require the approval of the Bundesrat. Since 2011 and 2014 the two smallest parties represented in the Bundestag, Alliance 90/The Greens and The Left party, have provided the Prime Minister in one federal state each (Baden-Wurttemberg and Thuringia respectively).

Because there is no uniform election date for the federal state parliaments and the legislature periods vary, parallel to the legislative term in the Bundestag the balance of power in the Bundesrat can change several times. With the current constellation of the chamber of federal states, the Federal Government has no safe majority in the Bundesrat. There are no longer any distinct blocks demonstrating uniform voting behaviour, as there is more diversity with regard to coalitions in the 16 federal states than ever before in the Federal Republic. Only in Bavaria can a single party, the CSU, rule without a coalition partner. Otherwise, in addition to federal state governments made up of the CDU and SPD parties there are also combinations of SPD and Alliance 90/The

Greens, of the CDU and Alliance 90/The Greens, of SPD and The Left party and one coalition of The Left party, SPD, and Alliance 90/The Greens.

The Federal President is the most senior political person in the country

In terms of protocol the Federal President holds the highest office. He is elected not by the people, but by a Federal Assembly convened specially for the purpose. Half of it is made up of the members of the Bundestag, the other half of members elected by the federal state parliaments in relation to the distribution of seats there. The Federal President holds office for five years and may be re-elected once. Joachim Gauck has been Federal President since 2012. He is not a member of any political party and was a Protestant pastor in the former East Germany. During the 1989-1990 peaceful revolution he was an active member of the civil rights movement. Joachim Gauck is the 11th Federal President since 1949. Although the Federal President's duties are primarily

☐ MILESTONES

1949
On 23 May the Parliamentary Council, which is made up of representatives of the states in the Western Occupation Zones, rresolves the Basic Law in Bonn. The first Bundestag is elected on 14 August.

1953
On 17 June 1953 around one million people take to the streets in East Berlin and East Germany in protest at the political and economic conditions. The uprising is quashed by a massive military operation.

1961
In Berlin, the East German leadership seals off the crossings from east to west: with a wall and barbed wire. Anyone henceforth seen trying to escape is shot. The unity of Germany as a state seems unattainable for the foreseeable future.

representational in nature, he can refuse to put his signature to legislation if he has doubts about it complying with the constitution. Previous incumbents have exerted the greatest influence through public speeches, which receive great attention. The Federal Presidents refrain from becoming involved in party politics, but do tackle current issues and from time to time urge the government, parliament, and the population to take action. Issues that Joachim Gauck, who refers to himself as the people's president, frequently addresses are human rights questions, Germany's responsibility for its actions, and dangers for democracy.

The Federal Constitutional Court in Karlsruhe: guardian of the Basic Law

The Federal Constitutional Court in Karlsruhe, which the population holds in very high esteem, exerts great influence. It is regarded as "the guardian of the Basic Law" and through its important decisions provides a binding interpretation of the constitutional text. In two panels it passes judgement on disputes between constitutional bodies about areas of jurisdiction, and can declare laws to be incompatible with the Basic Law. Any citizen can appeal to the Constitutional Court if he is of the opinion that a law violates his basic rights. The Federal Constitutional Court recently gained great importance through decisions relating to the assigning of Bundestag rights to the European Union. ∎

🌐 **GLOBAL**

Office for Democratic Institutions and Human Rights, Elections of the Federal Parliament (Bundestag) At the invitation of Germany, the Organization for Security and Co-operation in Europe (OSCE) observed the election of the Bundestag on 22 September 2013. In their report, the OSCE experts in particular address the new electoral law which was applied for the first time in the election, and which ensures that the distribution of seats in the Bundestag is more just. → osce.org

1969

Willy Brandt is the first Chancellor not to be a member of the CDU party. The Ostpolitik of the coalition government made up of the SPD and FDP creates a framework for the reconciliation of Germany with its eastern neighbours.

1989/90

In East Germany, peaceful protests lead to the regime being toppled. On 9 November the border with the West is opened. After the first free elections on 18 March, East Germany accedes to the Federal Republic on 3 October 1990.

1999

The Bundestag and the Federal Government are relocated to Berlin. The parliamentary buildings stand on both sides of the former course taken by the Wall. Bonn remains the seat of some ministries and federal authorities.

TOPIC
ACTIVE POLITICS

"Shaping Germany's Future" is the title the coalition parties chose for their four-year government programme. This shaping of the future includes budget planning, which on a long-term basis avoids requiring any new debt. This is intended to ensure Germany enjoys political freedom of action, even in times of economic crisis. With its objective of a balanced budget, which in both 2014 and 2015 it indeed achieved, the Federal Government considers itself responsible for monetary stability and wishes to be a role model for its partners in the Eurozone.

In the case of some of the government's major projects, there is support, in principle at least, from far beyond the coalition parties CDU/CSU and SPD. In early 2015, for example, a

※ NUMBER

0 euros

was what Germany's federal budget deficit came to in 2014. While expenditure totalled 296,500 million euros, revenue amounted to 296,500 million euros. This was an historic achievement on the part of the ruling Grand Coalition. For the first time in 45 years – since the 1969 budget – central government assumed no new debt.
→ bundeshaushalt-info.de

minimum wage of EUR 8.50 valid for all sectors was introduced for the first time; it will be reviewed regularly by a commission comprising representatives of the trade unions and entrepreneurs. Around 4 million people benefit from this new statutory minimum wage.

The introduction of a quota for women in large stock corporations likewise had widespread political support in parliament and the general public. From 2016, women must account for at least 30 percent of the members of these companies' supervisory boards, whereby the new regulation applies to 108 publicly listed firms that fall within the ambit of the German co-determination laws. In future, a further 3,500 companies will have to set themselves binding goals for increasing the proportion of women in executive positions. According to the German Institute for Economic Research (DIW), at the end of 2014 the share of women on the advisory boards of the 200 largest companies was 18.4 percent, meaning there is still ground to be made up.

The social policy projects in the current legislature include a "pension reform package", which among other things contains a mothers' pension that improves the social security of mothers who raised children born before 1992. A key part of the pension package is retirement at the age of 63. Since 1 July 2014 those people who have paid contributions into the state pension scheme for at least 45 years

The Bundestag in Berlin is the political stage. There are 630 members of the 18th German Bundestag

will be able to retire at the age of 63 without any deductions from their pension.

Germany is an attractive country for immigrants. In 2013 alone, more than 1.2 million people came to the country. To date, there are numerous different sets of statutory regulations that govern immigration and the process of political asylum. In the second half of the legislature, the Federal Government intends to agree on a simple, comprehensible body of laws, and in this way create a more streamlined procedure. Advancing the Energy Reform, through which Germany has already increased its share of regenerative energies to over 30 percent of total electricity consumption, as well as the expansion of the digital infrastructure are further focal points of forthcoming government activities. The parameters for these efforts are set out in the initial agreement reached between the coalition parties. ∎

TOPIC
BROAD PARTICIPATION

The political parties are granted a major and privileged place in the political system of the Federal Republic of Germany. Article 21 of the Basic Law states that "Political parties shall participate in the formation of the political will of the people." This goes hand in hand with an obligation to uphold inner-party democracy: The chairperson, committees, and candidates must all be elected by secret ballot of grass roots delegates at party conferences. In order to strengthen this inner-party democracy, in the case of important decisions parties have in recent times polled their members directly. The SPD members' vote on the Coalition Agreement in 2013 was pivotal to the forming of a joint Federal government with CDU/CSU. At heart the parties are still expressions of specific strata of society, but at the same time they are losing coherence in this regard. CDU/CSU and SPD together have around one million party members – in relation to almost 62 million eligible voters that is a share of 1.7 percent. There is also a downward trend in election turnout. Whereas in the 1970s and 1980s elections continually saw high and extremely high turnouts, (91.1 per cent in 1972), in 2009 and 2013 the elections to the Bundestag only saw turnouts of 70.8 and 71.5 percent respectively.

Young people often find being involved in local citizens' groups and non-government organisations more appealing. Social media are also becoming increasingly important as platforms for a specific type of political articulation and action. Citizens also participate directly in political issues through democratic procedures such as referendums. Over the past few years, there have been more opportunities for direct democracy at both federal state and municipal level, and citizens have made great use of these. ∎

〽 DIAGRAM   Downward trend: turnout in Bundestag elections (%)

The voice of the people
In Germany voting is on the basis of slightly modified personalised proportional representation. Every person eligible to vote has two votes. The first is for a party's candidate in the constituency, the second for a state list of candidates put up by a particular party. The second votes are the basis of the number of seats in the Bundestag.

1949	1972	1983	1990	2005	2013
78.5	91.1	89.1	77.8	77.7	71.5

Source: Federal Statistical Office

The instruments of direct democracy, such as referendums, come into play more frequently at the municipal level

Age structure of those entitled to vote

20.1 %
70 and older

3.6 %
18–21 years

12.5 %
21–30 years

13.6 %
60–70 years

13.2 %
30–40 years

18.7 %
50–60 years

18.3 %
40–50 years

Sources: Federal Statistical Office, returning officers of referendums

Turnout for referendums

Baden-Wurttemberg (2011)	**48.3** %
Berlin (2014)	**46.1** %
Hamburg (2010)	**39.3** %
Bavaria (2010)	**37.7** %

PANORAMA
POLITICAL BERLIN

❶ Bellevue Palace
Built in the late 18th century, Bellevue Palace has been the official residence of Germany's Federal President since 1994. It is located on the edge of Berlin's Tiergarten district.

❷ Federal Chancellery
The new Federal Chancellery went into service in 2001. The outside of the post-Modernist building is predominantly glazed. "Berlin", a steel sculpture by Basque artist Eduardo Chillida, is situated in the "Ehrenhof" (courtyard of honour).

630
MPs make up the
18th German Bundestag

36 %
of MPs in
the Bundestag
are women

62,000,000
Germans are eligible
to vote in elections to
the Bundestag

2,300,000
people visit the
Bundestag in Berlin
each year

Berlin
Mitte district

❶ Bellevue Palace
❷ Federal Chancellery
❸ German Bundestag
❹ Bundesrat
❺ Jakob Kaiser Building
❻ Paul Löbe Building
❼ Marie Elisabeth Lüders Building

River Spree

Strasse des 17. Juni

Tiergarten

❸ **German Bundestag**
The glass dome on the Reichstag building stands for transparency.

The Reichstag building
The German parliament sits in the modernised building dating from 1894.

14
ministers form the Cabinet

23
coalition governments since 1949

11
Federal Presidents since 1949

8
Federal Chancellors since 1949

TOPIC
VIBRANT CULTURE OF REMEMBRANCE

Addressing war and tyranny, ideologically motivated crimes and political injustice in the 20th century, not to mention commemorating the victims of persecution play an important role in the culture of remembrance in the Federal Republic of Germany. Preserving eye-witnesses reports by persons who actually experienced the events is the key element in a culture of remembrance destined to make certain that coming generations are conscious of the crimes committed by the Nazis. The numerous memorials to the various groups of victims all over Germany are also part of this vibrant culture of remembrance. In central Berlin, for example, the Memorial to the Murdered Jews of Europe is a memorial to the six million Jewish victims of the Holocaust.

The overwhelming sentiment in the memorial services in 2014 and 2015 marking the 100th anniversary of the beginning of the First World War and the 25th anniversary of the fall of the Berlin Wall was one of gratitude. Gratitude for the Allies' anti-Hitler coalition for liberating Germany in 1945, as well as for the opportunity to re-build the country and for it then to be re-united in 1990. There was also gratitude to those who, as surviving victims of the Holocaust, bore witness to the crimes – and reached out their hand to a democratic Germany after the Second World War. The initiation of diplomatic relations between Israel and Germany, the 50th anniversary of which was celebrated in 2015, was a particular symbol of this willingness to embrace reconciliation.

INFO

"Stolpersteine"
In many German and European cities, "Stolpersteine" (stumbling stones) placed in the ground remind passers-by that Jewish citizens who were persecuted, murdered, deported, or driven away by the Nazis, once lived or worked in the buildings outside which the stones are placed. The approximately 10 by 10-centimetre cube-shaped concrete blocks have a brass top with an inscription in memory of the victim bearing his or her name and biographical data.
→ stolpersteine.eu

Memorials to war, resistance and dictatorship

Memories of the communist dictatorship during the Soviet Occupation Zone (1945–1949) and the days of East Germany (1949–1990) are also being kept alive for those generations that never experienced the division of Germany and the East German system. The Federal Commissioner for the Records of the State Security Service of the Former German Democratic Republic, the institution where files are still being examined, sorted, and made accessible to those affected and academics, plays a major role in this.

MAP
Memorials in Germany

Memorials to the victims of Nazism

A permanent exhibition in the former head-quarters of the State Security Service (Stasi) of the German Democratic Republic in the Hohenschönhausen district of Berlin provides an insight into the means and methods of working the Stasi used to spy on, control, and intimidate the population. Exhibitions and lectures in the Stasi's former outposts in large East German cities keep memories of the dictatorship in the German Democratic Republic alive.

In the "Bendlerblock" in the Mitte district of Berlin the German Resistance Memorial Centre is devoted to the resistance to the Nazi dictatorship. It is located on the historical site of the failed coup attempted by the group headed by Count Stauffenberg on 20 July 1944. The Memorial Centre impressively documents how between 1933 and 1945 individuals and groups took action against the dictatorship of the Third Reich and made use of what freedom of action they had. ∎

FOREIGN POLICY

Civil Policy-Shaping Power •
Committed to Peace and Security • Advocate of European Integration •
Protection of Human Rights • Sustainable Development

INSIGHT
CIVIL POLICY-SHAPING POWER

On the international stage, Germany enjoys a very broad network of close contacts. It maintains diplomatic relations with almost 200 countries and is a member of all the important multilateral organisations and informal international coordination groups such as the "Group of Seven" (G7) and the "Group of Twenty" (G20). Dr. Frank-Walter Steinmeier (SPD) has been Federal Foreign Minister since 2013, having previously held the office from 2005 until 2009. The Federal Foreign Office, which is based in Berlin, has around 11,230 staff members. In total, Germany maintains 227 missions abroad.

The primary objective of German foreign policy is to ensure peace and security in the world. The basic premises on which it is based include the nation's full integration into the structures of multilateral cooperation. In concrete terms this means: close partnership with France in the European Union (EU), firm roots in the community of values shaped by the transatlantic alliance with the USA, support of the right of Israel to exist, active and committed involvement in the United Nations (UN) and the Council of Europe, as well as the strengthening of the European security structure through the OSCE.

Together with its partners, Germany promotes peace, security, democracy, and human rights all over the world. Alongside crisis prevention, disarmament, and arms control, the broad notion of security promulgated by Germany embraces sustainable economic, ecological, and social aspects. These include a globalisation that offers opportunities for everyone, cross-border environmental and climate protection, dialogue between cultures, and openness towards guests and immigrants.

▶

VIDEO ◳ AR APP

Foreign policy: the video on the topic
→ **tued.net/en/vid2**

German foreign policy is firmly embedded in multilateral cooperation

▸ **Since the end** of the East-West conflict, new opportunities and challenges have emerged for German foreign policy. On the basis of its multilateral relations, Germany has accepted the increased responsibility it has been accorded since reunification in 1990. Through its many efforts, Germany nowadays plays a role in the political resolution of conflicts, the maintenance of peace-keeping structures, and crisis prevention as part of UN-mandated peace missions. In the midst the current crisis in the European security order, in 2016 it will assume the Chairmanship of the OSCE and will promote an affirmation of the Helsinki Principles and a strengthening of the OSCE as the main regional security organisation in Europe.

The public discussion surrounding the "Review 2014 – A Fresh Look at German Foreign Policy" project revealed that the premises on which German foreign policy are based have proven their worth. However, it also showed that in a rapidly changing world German foreign policy faces three main challenges, which can be described with the words "Crisis – Order – Europe". In order to be better prepared to master them, and as a result of the review process, the Federal Foreign Office is being restructured.   ∎

→ INTERNET

Federal Foreign Office
Appointments, people, issues, contacts
→ diplo.de

European Union
Portal of the community of states with information in 24 languages
→ europa.eu

OSCE
Permanent mission of the Federal Republic of Germany to the OSCE
→ osze.diplo.de

Federal Foreign Minister Steinmeier (left) played a major role in the successful E3+3 talks with Iran

PLAYERS & ORGANISATIONS

Diplomatic missions
Germany maintains diplomatic relations with 195 countries and has a global presence with 227 missions, 153 of them embassies.
→ diplo.de

Multilateral organisations
Germany assumes responsibility in multilateral organisations such as the United Nations (UN), the European Union (EU), the North Atlantic Alliance (NATO), the Organization for Security and Co-operation in Europe (OSCE), the European Council, the Organisation for Economic Co-Operation and Development (OECD), the World Trade Organization (WTO), and the International Monetary Fund (IMF).

Foreign policy think tanks
Important foreign and security policy research institutes include the German Council on Foreign Relations (DGAP), the German Institute of Global and Area Studies (GIGA), the Peace Research Institute Frankfurt (PRIF), the Institute for Peace Research and Security Policy (IFSH), and German Institute for International and Security Affairs (SWP).

Bundeswehr
Following an internal reform the Bundeswehr now has around 180,000 active soldiers, of which 19,000 are women. In 2015, a total of 2,500 members of the German armed forces were deployed to missions in 16 different crisis areas.
→ bundeswehr.de

Political foundations
The foundations closely associated with the German political parties CDU, CSU, SPD, The Left party, Alliance 90/The Greens, and FDP have offices worldwide. With federal funds, they promote dialogue and development in partner countries.

Experts in conflict prevention
The Centre for International Peace Operations trains civilian specialists for missions in crisis regions and provides experts.
→ zif-berlin.org

➕ DIGITAL PLUS
More information about all the topics in the chapter – annotated link lists, articles, documents, speeches; plus more in-depth information about the European Union as well as short portraits of the multilateral organisations.
→ tued.net/en/dig2

TOPIC
COMMITTED TO PEACE AND SECURITY

Diplomacy, crisis prevention, and the peaceful settlement of conflicts are the primary tools of German foreign policy: The posting of civil servants, judges, public prosecutors, police officers, development workers and other civilians is just as much part and parcel of a comprehensive security policy as the Bundeswehr, the German army, participating in multinational peace missions. The determining feature of German foreign policy, close multilateral involvement, also applies, indeed particularly so for the use of military means. In principle, the Bundeswehr is deployed within the framework of collective security or defence systems. As such it is bound to the resolutions passed by the United Nations (UN), European Union (EU), and

NATO. Wherever possible, Bundeswehr missions abroad are always accompanied by a civilian component, such as political, development, and socio-economic measures. Missions involving armed forces are subject to parliamentary mandate and control. They need the express approval of a majority of the members of the German parliament, the Bundestag, and are in each case only for the duration of one year. For this reason, the Bundeswehr is also referred to as a parliamentary army.

Germany has been politically and militarily integrated in NATO since the Bundeswehr was first founded in 1955. Being firmly anchored in the North Atlantic defence alliance is part of German foreign policy's DNA. Germany is or was one of the biggest providers of troops for the NATO-led missions in Kosovo (KFOR) and Afghanistan (ISAF, Resolute Support). Since 1990 the Bundeswehr has been involved in 35 missions abroad, of which 19 were concluded by 2015.

In the wake of the Ukraine crisis, Germany once again demonstrated its commitment to NATO defence. In 2015 the Bundeswehr, together with the Netherlands and Norway, helped set up the NATO Very High Readiness Joint Task Force (VJTF), which as part of collective defence and crisis management is intended to improve the Alliance's

≡ LIST

• North Atlantic Treaty Organization (NATO), German accession in 1955

• United Nations (UN), German accession in 1973

• Organization for Security and Co-operation in Europe (OSCE), German accession on foundation in 1973 (at the time still the Conference on Security and Co-operation in Europe, CSCE)

The Bundeswehr is involved in numerous missions abroad, for example the European Training Mission in Mali (EUTM)

ability to respond swiftly. Since being admitted to the UN in 1973, the Federal Republic of Germany has been a committed, reliable, and valued member of the world organisation. For this reason, in 2018 Germany intends to stand as a candidate for one of the six non-permanent seats on the UN Security Council for the 2019-2020 term. Germany contributes around 190 million dollars annually to the regular UN budget, and some 640 million dollars to the separate budget for UN peace missions. In each case the figure is 7.1 percent of the total UN budget, making Germany the third biggest contributor in 2015. Around 260 German soldiers and police officers participated in UN-led missions in 2014, among others in Lebanon, Western Sahara, Mali, South Sudan, Sudan, and Liberia. The UN is present in Germany too, in particular on the UN Campus in Bonn, home to 19 of the 28 UN agencies in Germany as a whole, ▶

In 2016, Germany will be Chair of the OSCE, thus affirming its commitment to the organisation

▶ among them the UN Climate Secretariat (UNFCCC).

In order to better help international organisations on peace-keeping missions, Germany is going to put the training and deployment of civilian crisis response workers on an even more professional footing. Established in 2002, the Centre for International Peace Operations has a pool of 1,500 experts on call, and will be strengthened still further. It selects civilian crisis managers, prepares them on training courses for missions as observers and mediators in crisis areas and post-conflict countries, and evaluates their experiences. In cooperation with the Federal Foreign Office, by 2015 the Centre for International Peace Operations had already posted 3,000 short and long-term volunteers on election observation missions, and conducted projects in 65 countries.

Germany supports the Organization for Security and Co-operation in Europe (OSCE), another mainstay of peace and security in Europe. The organisation originated in the Conference on Security and Co-operation in Europe (CSCE) and adopted its present name in 1995. The core document of the OSCE is the Helsinki Final Act, which was signed in 1975, and in which, among other things, the inviolability of frontiers and the peaceful settlement of disputes were agreed as basic principles of the European security order.

The OSCE as the main forum for peace and security in Europe

Today the organisation has 57 participating states from Europe, North America and Central Asia making it the largest regional organisation for collective security worldwide. The importance of the OSCE as a central forum for dialogue and confidence building once again became clear during the Ukraine crisis. The OSCE supports the efforts for a peaceful settlement of the Ukraine conflict, among other things by conducting political negotiations in the Trilateral Contact Group.

Furthermore, the OSCE has deployed several hundred civilian observers to Ukraine to monitor the ceasefire set out in the Minsk agreements signed in September 2014 and February 2015, and to verify the withdrawal of troops and weapons, for example in the area of conflict in eastern Ukraine. For the purpose of preventing conflicts and promoting democratisation, the OSCE maintains permanent missions in several countries and, with the support of Germany, regularly sends election observers to its participating states.

Commitment to disarmament and arms control

Disarmament, arms control, and the non-proliferation of nuclear weapons have long since had a high priority in German foreign policy. Germany is committed to the goal of a world free of all nuclear weapons and to this end pursues a pragmatic approach. Together with the five permanent members of the UN Security Council, Germany played a constructive role in the E3+3 negotiations leading to the Vienna agreement with Iran on the Iranian nuclear programme. Germany continues to support the universality and enforcement of relevant international treaties and agreements. In 2014 and 2015 it was

closely involved in the destroying or rendering harmless various chemical weapons removed from Syria. Between 2013 and 2016 Germany will have conducted projects worth approximately 24 million euros in more than 20 partner countries aimed at improving security against biological weaponry of any kind. Furthermore, Germany has contributed around 13.2 million euros to projects for clearing mines and caring for mine victims, making it one of the biggest donors in this area. The destruction of superfluous weapons and munition and the safe storage of endangered stocks are focal points of German policy. Conventional arms control, as well as confidence and security-building measures are of enormous importance in the OSCE area. Germany is in favour of the relevant mechanisms being modernised and adapted to meet current challenges. ∎

🌐 **GLOBAL**

Armed Conflict Survey 2015 According to the International Institute for Strategic Studies (IISS) in London, the past few years have seen a considerable increase in the number of war victims. The number of war dead rose from 56,000 in 2008 to 180,000 in 2014, even though instead of 63 only 42 armed conflicts were counted. In 2013, for the first time since the end of the Second World War, more than 50 million people were refugees.
→ iiss.org

TOPIC
ADVOCATE OF EUROPEAN INTEGRATION

No country in Europe has more neighbours than Germany. It shares its border with nine countries, eight of which are European Union (EU) member states. For Germany, European integration, one of the most impressive political success stories of recent decades, lays the foundations for peace, security, and prosperity. Advancing and strengthening this, particularly in view of complex and in many cases crisis-ridden conditions, remains the main task of German foreign policy. Begun in the early 1950s, the historical project that today is the EU nowadays has over half a billion citizens in 28 member states. German European policy emerged as a driving force in all stages of European unification, and actively helped shape the process of European cohesion following the end of the East-West conflict. This European integration created the world's largest common market, characterised by the four fundamental freedoms formulated in the Treaty of Rome signed in 1957: the free movement of goods between the EU member states, the freedom of movement of persons, the freedom to provide services within the EU, and the free flow of capital.

The financial and debt crisis which took shape in 2008 left the European unification process facing major challenges. For this reason the banking union, which establishes common standards and control mechanisms for the financial sector in the Eurozone, was a key objective of German European policy. Social cohesion among Europeans, in difficult times as well, enjoys widespread support among the German population. The size and economic output of the common European market make the EU a major player in the global economy. The Eurozone alone accounts for more than a fifth of the gross domestic product generated worldwide – putting it in second place behind the USA. At the same time the Eurozone is the most important importer and exporter of goods and services worldwide. The IMF is expecting growth of 1.6 percent for 2016; in 2013, the European Economic Area was still in recession. As the strongest

NUMBER

508 million

people live in the 28 member states of the European Union. This gives it the third largest population after China and India. Its citizens speak 24 languages and live in an area covering four million square kilometres. GDP totals 13.92 trillion euros and is bigger than that of the USA. With a share of 15.4 percent of exports and 16.4 percent of imports, the EU leads the way in worldwide trade.
→ europa.eu

MAP

The 28 member states of the European Union at a glance

economy in the EU, Germany has a particular responsibility, not least of all at times of economic and social change.

Franco-German friendship – the driving force behind European unification

Parallel to European integration, after the Second World War France and Germany established a close partnership, which nowadays is often regarded as a model for reconciliation between two peoples. In 1957, both countries were among the six founding members of the European Economic Community (EEC), the core of today's EU. Franco-German friendship, substantiated by the 1963 Elysée Treaty, is nurtured by close relations between the civil societies and numerous Franco-German institutions. With regard to European and foreign policy issues, both countries cooperate closely and through joint initiatives repeatedly play a ▶

▶ role in constructively advancing European policy.

German-Polish collaboration is a more recent element in the European unification process. In the 1970s, Federal Chancellor Willy Brandt's Ostpolitik achieved initial successes in reconciliation with Poland. This was continued by the recognition of the two countries' common border in the Two Plus Four Treaty on the external aspects of German Unity in 1990, and with the Border Treaty concluded the same year and institutionalised in the 1991 German-Polish Treaty on Good Neighbourliness. The close relationships with France and Poland are nurtured in the trilateral format of the Weimar Triangle.

More global weight through joint European action

The 2009 Treaty of Lisbon institutionalised the Common Foreign and Security Policy (CFSP) still further. The EU High Representative for Foreign Affairs and Security Pol-

icy, who chairs the Council of Foreign Ministers, is also Vice-President of the European Commission. Italian Federica Mogherini has held this office since 2014. She is also responsible for representing the EU externally on all CFSP issues. A newly established European External Action Service (EEAS) assists the High Representative in discharging her duties. Through these institutional innovations the EU has considerably strengthened its visibility and efficacy outside its own territory. It has also advanced its crisis management. Under the aegis of the EU, several foreign assignments with German participation have already been conducted.

A focal point of EU policy is to foster relations with the organisation's eastern neighbours and the countries bordering eastern and southern Mediterranean rim. With regard to this Neighbourhood Policy, migration and the fight against terrorism are increasingly being prioritised. Irregular immigration to Europe is a pan-European issue. To this end, in April and June 2015, the European Council passed a comprehen-

🏛 **MILESTONES**

1957
The European unification process begins. The signing of the Treaties of Rome by Belgium, Germany, France, Italy, Luxembourg, and the Netherlands marks the foundation of the European Economic Community (EEC).

1979
Europeans vote together. The Members of the European Parliament, which sits in Strasbourg and Brussels, are directly elected for the first time. They had previously been delegated by the national parliaments.

1993
Europe's union becomes tangible for its citizens. In Schengen in Luxembourg, Germany, France and the Benelux countries agree to end internal border controls. Other countries follow.

The 2015 G7 Summit: European and global issues were on the agenda under the German G7 Presidency

sive programme of measures. In addition to increasing sea rescue operations in the Mediterranean and measures to fight the smuggling and trafficking of human beings, the fight against the causes of people fleeing from and irregular migration in their home countries and transit countries in Africa and the Middle East also plays a role. The question of the more uniform distribution of asylum seekers in the EU still requires a sustainable, fair answer. In 2014, five countries, and among them primarily Germany, absorbed two thirds of all refugees. No country in Europe took in more people from Syria: over 125,000. The solution the European Council reached in June 2015, of re-settling refugees in need of help within the EU on a voluntary basis rather than rigidly in line with country of first registration, is an initial step in this direction. ∎

2002

Europe gives itself a currency. In initially 12 EU member states, the cash euro is introduced; it had served as book money since 1999. The new European Central Bank (ECB) is based in Frankfurt am Main.

2004

On 1 May Estonia, Latvia, Lithuania, Poland, Czech Republic, Slovakia, Slovenia, Hungary, Malta, and Cyprus join the EU. Bulgaria and Romania follow three years later; Croatia in 2013.

2009

The EU presents a united front in the world. With the Treaty of Lisbon, the EU creates the office of the High Representative for Foreign Affairs and Security Policy. A European External Action Service (EEAS) is established.

TOPIC
PROTECTION OF HUMAN RIGHTS

"Human dignity shall be inviolable. To respect and protect it shall be the duty of all state authority." This is the clear mandate in Article 1 of the German Basic Law, in which Germany acknowledges "inviolable and inalienable human rights" as "the basis of every community, of peace and of justice in the world". Germany also takes this obligation seriously in its relations with foreign countries. The protection and strengthening of human rights play a special role in the foreign-policy and international context, as systematic human rights violations are frequently the first step towards conflicts and crises. Together with its partners in the EU and in collaboration with the United Nations (UN), Germany advocates the protection and improvement of human rights standards.

Commitment to international human rights institutions

Germany is a contracting partner to the UN's important human rights treaties and their Additional Protocols (Civil Pact, Social Pact, Anti-Racism Convention, Women's Rights Convention, Convention against Torture, Children's Rights Convention, Convention on the Rights of Persons with Disabilities, Convention for the Protection of All Persons from Enforced Disappearance). Most recently Germany signed the Additional Protocol to the Convention against Torture, and the Convention on the Rights of Persons with Disabilities, both of which have been in force since 2009. Germany was the first European nation to ratify the Additional Protocol to the Children's Rights Convention, which makes an individual complaints procedure possible.

The Federal Government supports protection from discrimination and racism, takes an active stand worldwide against the death penalty and for political participation and legal protection, defends the freedom of religion and belief, fights human trafficking, and pushes for enforcement of the right to housing and the right to clean water and sanitation. Almost 900 million people

ⓘ **INFO**

Civil Society The many non-government organisations in Germany also champion the global enforcement of human rights, progress in development policy, and humanitarian assistance. They encourage the politicians responsible to take action and raise awareness for such activities among the population. But they also take active steps themselves, collect donations and co-ordinate projects of their own. Around 120 organisations make up VENRO, the umbrella organisation of non-governmental development organisations.
→ venro.org

The Human Rights Council in Geneva is the United Nations' most important human rights committee

worldwide have no access to clean water. Germany is helping to change this situation by spending 400 million euros annually on several projects. Access to water, one of the more recent human rights issues, is the focal point of German development cooperation in 27 countries.

In 2012, Germany became a member of the UN Human Rights Council in Geneva, Switzerland, for the second time, and is currently applying to be re-elected for the 2016–2018 cycle. In 2015, Germany in the person of Ambassador Joachim Rücker became Chair of the Council for the first time. The German diplomat was elected President by the 47 members of the Human Rights Council for one year. The Human Rights Council's most important tool is the Universal Periodic Review, which provides all UN member states with an opportunity to declare what actions they have taken to fulfil their human rights ▶

▶ obligations, and answer critical questions. Germany underwent this procedure in 2009 and 2013.

Germany is one of the most active countries on the European Council, which has 47 member states and champions the protection and promotion of human rights, the rule of law, and democracy throughout Europe. With landmark conventions, in particular the European Human Rights Convention, the European Council plays a strong role in establishing a common European judicial area and monitors adherence to binding common standards and values on the European continent.

International human rights policy tools

The European Court of Human Rights (ECtHR) in Strasbourg, France is one of the European Council's main institutions for enforcing human rights in Europe. Each and every citizen of the 47 member states of the European Council can resort directly to the ECtHR with complaints concerning a violation of rights protected by the European Human Rights Convention. Germany emphatically advocates that all member states of the European Council accept and implement the decisions of the ECtHR, as is incumbent upon them. The International Criminal Court (ICC) in The Hague, the Netherlands, is responsible for the prosecution under international criminal law of serious international crimes such as war crimes, crimes against humanity, and genocide. Germany is in favour of universal recognition of the ECtHR.

The Federal Government Commissioner for Human Rights Policy and Humanitarian Aid, Christoph Strässer, is based in the Federal Foreign Office. He observes international developments, coordinates human rights activities with other state bodies, and advises the Federal Foreign Minister. The German parliament, the Bundestag, has accompanied and monitored German human rights policy

〰️ **D I A G R A M**

Spending on government development cooperation in USD billion

Cooperation and development
Germany is not only one of the important and major donor countries in the field of government development cooperation; it is also an important donor for, and actively helps shape humanitarian aid.

USA	**32.73**
Great Britain	**19.39**
Germany	**16.25**
France	**10.37**
Japan	**9.19**

Source: OECD / DAC

since 1998 through its Committee for Human Rights and Humanitarian Aid. In 2000, the German Institute for Human Rights, a state-funded but independent body, was established in Berlin. As a national human rights institution as defined in the UN's Paris Principles, it is intended to help the promotion and protection of human rights by Germany at home and abroad.

Humanitarian aid for people in acute need

Through its humanitarian aid worldwide the Federal Government helps people in acute need as a result of natural disasters, armed conflicts, or other crises and conflicts – or where there is a risk of this becoming the case. It is not about the causes of their plight. Humanitarian aid is an expression of ethical responsibility and solidarity with people in need. It is geared to the requirements of the needy and is based on the humanitarian principles of humanity, neutrality, impartiality, and independence.

The Federal Government does not provide this assistance directly, but supports suitable projects conducted by the UN's humanitarian organisations, the Red Cross and Red Crescent Movement, and German non-government organisations. In 2014 alone, the Federal Foreign Office allocated in excess of 437 million euros for humanitarian measures.

The protection of human rights is also an important field of activity for cyber foreign policy. Issues relating to the protection of data and privacy rights need urgent answers. In 2013 and 2014, the UN General Assembly passed resolutions on the right to privacy in the digital age. They were on the back of a German-Brazilian initiative. Germany is of the opinion that human rights online are just as valid as offline. In 2015, the UN Human Rights Council adopted a resolution that for the first time envisages the appointment of an independent special reporter for the right to privacy. He will report on violations annually and follow the international debate. ∎

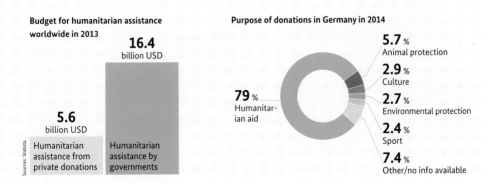

Budget for humanitarian assistance worldwide in 2013

16.4 billion USD

5.6 billion USD

Humanitarian assistance from private donations

Humanitarian assistance by governments

Sources: Statista

Purpose of donations in Germany in 2014

79 % Humanitarian aid

5.7 % Animal protection

2.9 % Culture

2.7 % Environmental protection

2.4 % Sport

7.4 % Other/no info available

🖵 PANORAMA
OPEN NETWORK PARTNER

New York
- United Nations headquarters

Montreal
- United Nations

Washington, D.C.
- International Monetary Fund (IMF)
- World Bank

Luxembourg
- EU

London
- United Nations

Strasbourg
- EU

Madrid
- United Nations

Paris
- United Nations
- European Space Agency (ESA)
- Organisation for Economic Co-operation and Development (OECD)

Brussels
- NATO
- EU

Stockholm
- Council of the Baltic Sea States

Vienna
- OSCE

Bern
- United Nations

Rome
- United Nations

Geneva
- United Nations
- World Trade Organization (WTO)

Nairobi
- United Nations

New York
United Nations headquarters

Geneva
Seat of the World Trade Organization

IWF
Germany has been a member of the International Monetary Fund since 1952

NATO
Germany has been a member of the North Atlantic Treaty Organization since 1955

EU
Germany has been a member of what is today the EU since it was founded in 1957

UN
Germany became a member of the United Nations in 1973

The United Nations (UN) in Germany

● Hamburg
● Berlin
Dresden ●
● Bonn
● Frankfurt
● Nuremberg

Berlin
· International Labour Organization (ILO) –
  office in Germany
· The United Nations High Commissioner for
  Refugees (UNHCR) – Regional Representation
  for Germany and Austria
· World Food Programme (WFP) –
  liaison office in Germany
· Office of the World Bank in Berlin

Bonn UN Campus
· United Nations Volunteers (UNV)
· Climate Change Secretariat (UNFCCC)
· Secretariat of the United Nations Convention
  to Combat Desertification (UNCCD)
· International Strategy for Disaster Reduction/
  Platform for the Promotion of Early Warning
  (UN/ISDR-PPEW)
· United Nations University Vice Rectorate in
  Europe (UNU-ViE)
· and 14 other UN agencies

Dresden
· United Nations University – Institute for
  Integrated Management of Material Fluxes
  and of Resources (UNU-FLORES)

Frankfurt am Main
· International Finance Corporation (IFC),
  World Bank Group

Hamburg
· International Tribunal for the Law of the Sea
  (ITLOS)
· UNESCO Institute for Lifelong Learning (UIL)

Nuremberg
· UNHCR sub-office

Shima
· Japanese G7
  Presidency, 2016

Shanghai
· Chinese G20
  Presidency, 2016

Strasbourg
European
Parliament

Hamburg
International Tribunal
for the Law of the Sea

Bonn
The "Tall Eugene" building
on the UN Campus

OSCE
Germany has been
a member of what
is today the OSCE
since 1975

G7
Germany has been a
member of the informal
bloc since it was founded
in 1975

WTO
Germany has been a member
of the World Trade
Organization since 1995

G20
Germany has been a
member of the Group of
Twenty since it was
founded in 1999 in Berlin

TOPIC
SUSTAINABLE DEVELOPMENT

German development policy is geared as a cornerstone of a global structural and peace policy to helping improve living conditions in partner countries. It aims to overcome hunger and poverty worldwide and strengthen democracy and the rule of law. The Federal Ministry of Economic Cooperation and Development draws up the guidelines and concepts. Politically and financially, the main emphasis is on bilateral cooperation with partner countries. As part of government development cooperation, Germany works with 50 partner countries in jointly agreed country programmes that can involve all the various government tools for development cooperation. Africa is a key region, but Germany also works extremely closely with countries in Asia, southeast Europe, and Latin America.

Germany has increased the budget for development cooperation by 8.3 billion euros through 2019. This means that in 2016 a good 0.4 percent of the gross domestic product will be channelled into development cooperation. On an international scale, the 16.25 billion dollars Germany allocates annually puts it third among the largest donor countries for public development cooperation, behind the USA and Great Britain. As a rule, Deutsche Gesellschaft für Internationale Zusammenarbeit (GIZ) and the KfW Group are the implementing organisations and manage the projects in the various countries.

Global development in the coming years will be decisively influenced by the 2030 Agenda as resolved by the 70th Session of the UN General Assembly at the end of September 2015. The 2030 Agenda will replace the United Nations' Millennium Development Goals, which defined development in developing and emerging nations for the period 2000 to 2015, and indeed go far beyond them.

The 2030 Agenda for Sustainable Development

Even though by 2015 efforts in pursuit of the Millennium Development Goals had succeeded in halving starvation worldwide and, among other things, improving access to drinking water and education, almost 1.3 billion people live on less than 1.25 dollar a day. Other problems such as the overly great use of resources, ongoing climate change and the destruction of the environment, high unemployment and social inequality, likewise remain urgent.

The new September 2015 goals are intended to boost a worldwide change in favour of more sustainability – in the economic, ecological, and social dimensions, and taking the existing links between the three into consideration. From now on the idea is for there to be a "universal" agenda, in other words one applicable to all countries. The

The United Nations' 2030 Agenda aims to advance sustainable development in important areas for the future

focus in the coming 15 years is on addressing a broad range of policies that go far beyond development cooperation: In addition to the fight against starvation and poverty, planet Earth, as the basis of existence of future generations, will be protected; economic systems and lifestyles will become more just and more sustainable (as well as more efficient), discrimination will be fought, not least of all by strengthening effective inclusive and democratic institutions, responsible governance, as well as the rule of law.

Ultimately the agreement for ensuring sustainability in the future needs a "multiplayer" approach: The plan envisages that in addition to governments, social groups and the worlds of business and scholarship will play important roles in the implementation of the 2030 Agenda. ∎

BUSINESS & INNOVATION

A Strong Hub • Global Player •
Lead Markets and Innovative Products • Sustainable Economy •
Digital Agenda • Attractive Labour Market

INSIGHT

A STRONG HUB

Germany is the largest economy in the European Union (EU) and the fourth largest in the world after the USA, China, and Japan. The German economy has its great innovativeness and strong focus on exports to thank for its competitiveness and global networking. In high-selling sectors, such as car-making, mechanical and plant engineering, the chemicals industry and medical technology, exports account for far more than half of total sales. In 2014, only China and the USA exported more goods. Germany invests around 80 billion euros annually in research and development (R&D). Many companies are well on the way to "Industry 4.0", a project destined in particular to advance digitalisation in production engineering and logistics.

The positive economic momentum has led to a favourable trend on the labour market. Germany is one of the countries with the highest employment rates in the EU and is the country with the lowest youth unemployment percentage. This underscores the value of dual vocational training, which has become an export commodity in its own right and is being adapted by many countries. Factors such as the availability of skilled labour, infrastructure and legal certainty are further characteristics of Germany, which is very high on the list in many international rankings. Federal Deputy Chancellor Sigmar Gabriel (SPD) is likewise Federal Minister for Economic Affairs and Energy.

Since 1949 the idea of a social market economy has formed the basis of German economic policy. The social market economy guarantees free entrepreneurial activity while at the same time endeavouring to create social checks and balances. Formulated in the post-War years by Ludwig Erhard, who ▶

VIDEO ◯ AR APP

Business & Innovation: the video on
the topic → **tued.net/en/vid3**

Industry 4.0: the economy in Germany is fast en route to the digitalised future

▸ was later to become Federal Chancellor, the concept has kept Germany's economic development on a successful track. Germany actively engages in shaping globalisation and champions a sustainable global economic system, which offers fair opportunities to everyone.

Germany is one of the 12 countries which introduced the euro in 2002. The financial market crisis (2008) and the subsequent debt crisis affected the whole of the Eurozone, Germany included. To combat adverse impacts, the Federal Government employed a twin-track strategy, which involved not taking on any new debt and adopting measures to bolster innovativeness. For the first time since 1969, in 2014 and 2015 the government was able to present a balanced federal budget.

Accounting for more than 99 percent of all companies, small and medium-sized enterprises (SMEs) are the backbone of the economy.

They supplement the corporations listed primarily on the DAX index at the Frankfurt Stock Exchange, the most important financial centre in Continental Europe. The European Central Bank, which as an EU institution among other things guards the euro's price stability, is also headquartered in Frankfurt am Main.   ■

→ INTERNET

Federal Ministry for Economic Affairs and Energy
Economic policy, priority issues, initiatives
→ bmwi.de

Make it in Germany
Info portal for international skilled workers
→ make-it-in-germany.de

Employment Agency
Labour market data and job vacancies
→ arbeitsagentur.de

Financial centre with a long-standing tradition: Frankfurt am Main is Germany's most important stock exchange

PLAYERS & ORGANISATIONS

Federation of German Industries

The Federation of German Industries (BDI) represents the interests of over 100,000 industrial companies. It has an extensive network in all important markets and in international organisations.
→ **bdi.eu**

German Chambers of Commerce Abroad

The German Chambers of Commerce Abroad (AHK), delegations and representative offices of German industry and commerce form a network with 130 locations in 90 countries.
→ **ahk.de**

German diplomatic missions

The 227 embassies and consulates, together with the AHK and Germany Trade and Invest (GTAI), are the third pillar in the promotion of foreign trade.
→ **auswaertiges-amt.de**

Association of German Chambers of Commerce and Industry

The Association of German Chambers of Commerce and Industry (DIHK) is the umbrella organisation of the 80 German Chambers of Commerce and Industry; a total of 3.6 million commercial enterprises are members.
→ **dihk.de**

German Institute for Economic Research

The German Institute for Economic Research (DIW) in Berlin is the biggest of the numerous German economic research institutes.
→ **diw.de**

Germany Trade and Invest

Germany Trade and Invest (GTAI) is the economic development agency of the Federal Republic of Germany. With over 50 locations worldwide it helps German companies set up operations abroad, promotes Germany as a business and technology location and helps foreign companies settle in Germany.
→ **gtai.de**

Council for Sustainable Development

Appointed by the Federal Government, the Council for Sustainable Development is responsible among other things for developing measures to implement the National Sustainability Strategy.
→ **nachhaltigkeitsrat.de**

+ DIGITAL PLUS

More information about all the topics in the chapter – annotated link lists, articles, documents, speeches; plus more in-depth information about topics such as the social market economy, dual vocational training, economic policy, the European economic, and financial crisis. → **tued.net/en/dig3**

TOPIC
GLOBAL PLAYER

Germany is an industrialised nation with strong international links and a pronounced export focus. In the annual World Trade Organization (WTO) rankings, Germany regularly places among the three largest exporters behind China and the USA. In 2014, the foreign trade balance closed with a surplus of 190 billion euros, a new record. Exports by German companies (goods and services) increased to 1,326 billion euros, with the value of imports totalling 1,136 billion euros. With the global economy if anything posting low overall growth in 2013-4, the German economy performed well. Compared with other countries, Germany is benefitting most from globalisation. The McKinsey Global Institute "Country Connectedness Index 2014" lists Germany as the best-networked country worldwide – ahead of the USA and Singapore.

Every second euro earned in Germany is generated through an international business transaction. Almost one job in four is dependent on exports; in industry it is even one in two. Around 800,000 companies engage in foreign trade. In 2014, 685,000 corporations imported goods from other countries, while approximately 340,000 were busy as exporters. Some 10,700 firms domiciled outside Germany played a significant role in German foreign trade; the Association of German Chambers of Commerce and Industry (DIHK) estimates that more than 7 million employees work for German companies abroad.

In terms of exports, the emphasis is on motor vehicles and automotive components, machines, chemical products, and IT appliances and electronic products. These four product groups account for a good half of German exports. Overall, the export ratio has since 1991 almost doubled, rising from 25.7 percent to 50.6 percent. In 2013 the ▶

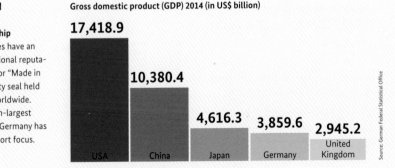

◢ DIAGRAM

Economic leadership
German companies have an excellent international reputation. They stand for "Made in Germany", a quality seal held in high esteem worldwide. The world's fourth-largest economic power, Germany has a pronounced export focus.

Gross domestic product (GDP) 2014 (in US$ billion)

17,418.9 — USA
10,380.4 — China
4,616.3 — Japan
3,859.6 — Germany
2,945.2 — United Kingdom

Source: German Federal Statistical Office

Containers – a symbol of globalisation: Hamburg docks is a major transhipment point

The world's largest trading nations in 2014 (share of world exports)

12.4% China

8.6% USA

8.0% Germany

3.6% Japan

3.6% Netherlands

Source: F.A.Z. newspaper, WTO

Largest German companies in 2014 (sales in € million)

Volkswagen	202,458
Daimler AG	129,872
Eon SE	111,556
BMW Group	80,401
Schwarz Group	79,300
BASF Group	74,326
Siemens AG	71,920

► foreign trade ratio, i.e., the sum total of imports and exports in relation to the gross domestic product (GDP), stood at 89 percent. This makes Germany's economy the "most open" of the G7 countries. By way of comparison, in 2013 the USA had a foreign trade ratio of 30 percent.

The partner countries in the European Union (EU) are the most important market for German goods and attract 58 percent of all exports. France is traditionally Germany's largest export market, though in the first six months of 2015 the USA headed the list for the first time, followed by Great Britain, the People's Republic of China and the Netherlands. With regard to imports, however, the rankings run the other way round: In 2014 most imports came from the Netherlands, followed by the People's Republic of China, France, the USA, and Italy. Although in some cases growth rates are weakening, nevertheless economic and trade relations with Asian countries are becoming ever more important and today 5,000 German companies have investments in China alone.

German direct investments abroad, which since 1990 have increased fivefold to 919 billion euros (2013), are an expression of its strong links within the global economy. A third of the total was invested in Euroland. Conversely, through their stake in local companies, foreign investors are responsible for 3 million jobs in Germany, with the value of foreign direct investments standing at 458 billion euros. This makes

🌐 **GLOBAL**

OECD Economic Outlook Twice a year in its Economic Outlook, the Organisation for Economic Co-operation and Development (OECD) analyses the most important trends and the prospects for the next two years in the 34 OECD member countries and emerging nations. The overall assumption for 2015-6 is that growth in the global economy will gain in momentum, but will be restrained in comparison with pre-crisis days.
→ oecd.org

Germany the seventh largest destination for investments.

The trade-fair industry is regarded as the hub of world trade. Germany is the leading trade fair centre when it comes to organising and staging international trade fairs. Two thirds of globally important industry events are held in Germany. Every year, 10 million visitors attend around 150 international trade fairs and exhibitions.

At the same time Germany is a transhipment hub for the flow of goods in Europe and the world as a whole. More goods transit through Germany than through any other EU country. About a third of the turnover in the ten most important logistics markets in the EU is generated in Germany, with 3 million people involved in logistics.

The Port of Hamburg, where around 9.7 million standard containers are processed each year, is a gateway to the world.

Commitment to fair and free global trade

Germany supports open markets and fair, free trade based on clear and reliable regulations. Among other things, the country pursues these goals with the three pillars for the promotion of foreign trade. These include 227 German diplomatic missions abroad, 130 German Chambers of Commerce Abroad (AHK), delegations and representative offices of the German economy in 90 countries, and Germany Trade and Invest (GTAI), the economic development agency of the Federal Republic of Germany. They all help small and medium-sized enterprises penetrate new markets and endeavour to improve framework conditions.

Germany is involved in shaping globalisation in various ways, be it through formulating regulations for international trade, regulating financial markets, or managing cash and foreign currency. Given faltering multilateral negotiations (the Doha Development Round), close attention is being paid to bilateral EU free trade agreements. Primarily, extensive treaties with the USA (Transatlantic Trade and Investment Partnership, TTIP) and Japan are currently under negotiation. The EU-Canada Comprehensive Economic and Trade Agreement (CETA) has been freshly negotiated. The EU Free Trade Agreement with South Korea, the first with an Asian country, has been in force since 2011; since that time exports to South Korea have risen each year by some 10 percent. In 2015 the EU and Vietnam adopted a free trade agreement, the first of its kind between the EU and a developing country. ∎

Global market hubs: as many as 10 million visitors attend the major trade fairs annually

TOPIC
LEAD MARKETS AND INNOVATIVE PRODUCTS

Germany's economic prowess is decidedly based on its industrial performance and its capacity for innovation. With 775,000 jobs, the automotive industry in particular is regarded as a showcase discipline with regard to the Made in Germany seal of quality. With its six strong brands, namely Volkswagen, BMW, Daimler, and the VW-owned marques Audi and Porsche, as well as Opel (General Motors), the automotive industry is one of the forces driving the global mobility sector.

The companies invest billions in research and development (R&D) to shore up their competitive edge. Electronic and digital networking, as well as assisted or self-driving cars, are the megatrends for automobiles. In global terms, in 2014 the German carmakers, which have a major share in the middle and luxury car segments, produced some 14.9 million cars, and the German automotive industry's export ratio is in excess of 77 percent.

Alongside the automotive industry, plant and mechanical engineering and the chemical industry are traditionally strong pillars of the German economy. Founded in 1865 and headquartered in Ludwigshafen, BASF, which has a payroll of 113,000 employees working at 390 production sites in more than 80 countries, is the world's largest chemicals company. Key sectors also include the electrical and electronic engineering industry, with global player Siemens active in 190 countries. Its application solutions, from medical technology to renewable energies, are regarded as highly innovative. The fact that the major sectors of industry achieve export ratios of 60 percent and more indicates just how important the global market is for them.

The most important economic centres in Germany are the Ruhr Area, Greater Munich and Greater Stuttgart (high-tech, automotive construction), Rhine-Neckar (chemicals, IT), Frankfurt am Main (finance), Cologne (media) and Hamburg (port, aircraft construction). In east Germany, small but efficient high-tech centres have emerged, in particular in the "beacon regions" of Dresden, Jena, Leipzig, Leuna, and Berlin-Brandenburg.

Automotive groups head and dominate the list of the biggest German companies (by 2014 sales): Volkswagen comes first, with Daimler and BMW following in second and fourth place respectively. Eon (energy) is in third place, BASF (chemicals) sixth, and Siemens (electrotechnology) seventh. Retail groups place fifth, eighth and ninth, while Deutsche Telekom places tenth.

Industry in Germany specialises in the development and manufacture of complex goods, in particular capital goods and

Successful the world over: German car manufacturers are among the big players in the global mobility sector

innovative production technologies. Industry carries far more weight in Germany than in many other economies. A total of 7.22 million people work in industry and manufacturing. Only in South Korea is the share of manufacturing in gross value added higher.

The economy's capacity for innovation is regarded as the driving force behind Germany's economic strength. The step-up in R&D activities since 2007 has spurred trends. Both business and the public sector played a role in this; the Federal Government's High-Tech Strategy has been a key stimulus here. In 2013 a total of almost 80 billion euros was spent on R&D in Germany, which corresponds to a 2.84-percent share of gross domestic product (GDP). This puts Germany in fifth place among comparable OECD countries, ahead of the USA and well ahead of France and Great Britain. Of Germany's main rivals, only South ▶

▶ Korea and Japan invested more in R&D. Germany is considered to be Europe's champion inventor. In 2014 German companies filed around 32,000 applications for patent protection to the European Patent Office in Munich. The same year, 65,958 inventions were registered with the German Patent and Trade Mark Office (DPMA) – a new record. The automotive supplier Bosch, with 4,000 registrations, and the Schaeffler Group (2,518), which likewise operates in the automotive components sector, were the most prolific. In total there were exactly 116,702 German patents in force in 2014. Moreover, 458,042 industrial property rights applicable to Germany were granted, the applications for which were processed by the European Patent Office.

Today, it is hard to imagine Germany as an industrial centre without its services economy, which has long been on a constant growth curve. A good 80 percent of all companies operate in this sector, accounting for almost 70 percent of gross domestic product, and three quarters of all jobs. Of around 30 million people in gainful employment, 12 million work for public or private service providers, almost 10 million in retailing, hospitality and transportation, and more than five million for corporate service providers.

Small and medium-sized enterprises – the heart of the economy

Despite the numerous global players and large flagship businesses, the German economy is characterised by 3.6 million small and medium-sized enterprises (SMEs), as well as countless self-employed persons and freelancers. The SME segment includes around 99.6 percent of companies. SMEs are defined as firms with annual sales of less than 50 million euros and fewer than 500 employees. Numerous companies founded by entrepreneurially minded migrants now also enjoy SME status. More than 700,000 people with a migrant background own a company. As such, migrants in Germany are an important economic factor.

🔲 **MILESTONES**

1955
On 5 August the one millionth VW Beetle leaves the assembly line in Wolfsburg. An absolute top seller, the car becomes a symbol of what went down in history as the Economic Miracle.

1969
In Toulouse (France) the Airbus consortium is founded as a Franco-German joint venture. Today, Airbus S.A.S. is the world's second-largest aircraft manufacturer.

1989
Postal Reform I marks the beginning of the privatisation of the giant publicly-owned corporation that is Deutsche Bundespost. The privatisation is regarded as one of the biggest reforms in German economic history.

According to studies by the KfW Banking Group, overall there is a decline in the number of innovative companies – only 28 percent of SMEs invest in innovative products and processes; one reason given for this is ongoing subdued economic forecasts. In numerous niche market segments, German SMEs are frequently hidden champions, with leaders offering highly innovative products in European and global markets. The creative industry has become firmly established in the fabric of the economy. Frequently in small, under-capitalised companies it plays a pioneering role on the way to a digital, knowledge-based economy, and is regarded as a significant source of ideas for innovative products. With more than 28,000 such firms registered, Berlin is considered to be an international seedbed for creative industries and start-ups.

The economy is on the threshold of the fourth industrial revolution. Driven by the Internet, the real and virtual worlds are growing together to create an Internet of Things. The Federal Government's aim is for the economy and scientists alike to support the implementation of Industry 4.0 and in so doing position Germany as a leading provider of these technologies and as a future manufacturing hub. ∎

ℹ INFO

Corporate tax rates
Since the mid-1990s there has been an international trend towards falling corporate tax rates. Germany has long since not been among the high-tax countries. In comparison with other countries, if anything, it even has below-average tax and welfare contribution levels. The average overall tax burden for companies is less than 30 percent. On account of the locally variable trade tax rate, in some regions in Germany it is below 23 percent.
→ gtai.de

1990
The Treuhandanstalt, a government-owned but independent trust agency, begins transforming the socialist planned economy of the former East Germany with its several thousand state-owned enterprises into a market economy.

2002
From 1948 until 1998 the Deutsche Mark is the official currency as "book money", until 2001 as cash. It is replaced on 1 January 2002: Germany and 11 other EU Member States introduce the euro.

2014
The German share index DAX passes the 10,000-point mark for the first time. It reflects the performance of the 30 biggest German companies with the highest sales.

TOPIC
SUSTAINABLE ECONOMY

Germany is one of the world's most sustainable industrialised nations. This is the conclusion reached by an international comparative study of the 34 OECD member states conducted by the Bertelsmann Foundation in 2015. Against the backdrop of the United Nations' 17 Sustainable Development Goals, the countries were systematically analysed for the first time on the basis of 34 indicators ranging from environmental protection and growth to the quality of the welfare systems. Germany was in sixth place, doing well in particular with regard to growth, employment and social security.

A growing number of companies in Germany are making a commitment to society

≡ LIST

- Largest company:
  Volkswagen, 592,586 employees

- Biggest bank:
  Deutsche Bank, 98,138 employees

- Most important stock market index:
  Deutscher Aktienindex (DAX)

- Largest trade fair grounds:
  Hanover

- Biggest aircraft manufacturer:
  Airbus, Hamburg

as part of conducting sustainable business. Corporate social responsibility (CSR) primarily hinges on each company's core business, which by dint of globalisation impacts on economic, social and environmental conditions. Most DAX-listed companies such as BASF, Daimler, and Deutsche Bank, as well as many SMEs, institutes and non-governmental organisations in Germany are members of the United Nations' Global Compact Initiative, founded in 1999. The latter, together with the OECD Guidelines for Multinational Enterprises and the International Labour Organisation's Tripartite Declaration of Principles concerning Multinational Enterprises and Social Policy, form the bedrock of principles on which companies base their CSR efforts. Worldwide, over 8,000 companies and 4,000 organisations are members of the voluntary Global Compact Initiative.

At the European level, Germany in particular supports the EU's far-reaching CSR initiative. The strategy is updated regularly and from 2016 envisages the introduction of obligatory reporting on CSR measures for certain companies. During Germany's presidency of the G7 in 2015, the Federal Government put CSR topics such as labour, welfare and environmental standards on the agenda.

The fact that social and ecological responsibility go hand in hand also becomes evident

Decent work: more and more German companies are placing importance on fair standards in global delivery chains

in the "Alliance for Sustainable Textiles", which seeks to achieve improvements on both counts for those employed in the textile and clothing industry. More than 100 German textile manufacturers, including the big players, have joined the initiative launched by the Federal Ministry for Economic Cooperation and Development (BMZ) in 2014. Through the Alliance, Germany aims to document its pioneering role with regard to international efforts for fair standards in global delivery chains.

For the purpose of formulating a CSR strategy, in 2009 the Federal Government convened a German CSR Forum and in 2010 the "National Strategy for Corporate Social Responsibility – CSR Action Plan" was concluded. One of its focal points is the successful implementation of CSR in small and medium-sized enterprises. ■

TOPIC
DIGITAL AGENDA

The economy is on the threshold of a fourth industrial revolution. Driven by the Internet, through a digital transformation process the real and virtual worlds are becoming increasingly intertwined and together form an Internet of Things. Digitalisation represents an historic change for industry and the service economy. The collective term Industry 4.0 embraces solutions, processes and technologies and describes the extensive use of IT and a high degree of system networking in factories. Many German companies are fast moving down the path to Industry 4.0, which in particular advances digitalisation in the areas of production engineering and logistics. Overall, industry is expecting ever intense international competition for leadership in technology. The Federal Government is promoting and actively shaping digital change, and to this end has established a Digital Agenda covering seven fields for action. It embraces all areas of society: government, industry, culture, education and science. Digital change is regarded not as purely technological, but as a social process that addresses questions of freedom and democracy, down to the protection of individuals.

In the medium term, the Digital Agenda is intended to make Germany the leading provider of Industry 4.0 and the number-one digital growth country in Europe. In positive scenarios, studies estimate additional economic growth potential from Industry 4.0 of between 200 and 425 billion euros by 2025. As a cross-cutting technology, the information and communications technology (ICT) sector plays a key role here. Today as much as 23 percent of growth in productivity can be traced to investment in ICT. 900,000 employees generate sales of 228 billion euros, making Germany the fourth-largest market after the USA, Japan and China, and the largest ICT market in Europe.

The development of the digital infrastructure, in particular of broadband Internet access, is regarded as one of the key tasks to drive digitalisation. The aim is to create a

NUMBER

600

Internet service providers and other organisations from 60 countries are linked up to DE-CIX. In terms of data throughput, the Internet hub in Frankfurt am Main is the largest in the world. In 2015 data throughput reached the 4-Terabit-per-second mark for the first time. After Marseille (France), Palermo (Italy) and Dallas (USA), the DE-CIX operator is now setting up a hub in Istanbul (Turkey).
→ de-cix.net

Always online: developing the digital infrastructure is among the Federal Government's key projects

nationwide broadband infrastructure with a download speed of at least 50 Mbit/s by 2018. The Federal Government and industry have put together an extensive 10-billion-euro broadband expansion package. That said, 87 percent of private households already have broadband access. Nonetheless there continue to be differences in broadband coverage between old and new federal states, and between cities and rural areas.

In 2015 broadband Internet with a speed of at least 50 Mbit/s, for the most part via landline, is available for almost two thirds of all households (64 percent). Connections with over 50 Mbit/s are available for four out of five (82 percent) households in cities, and for every fifth household (20 percent) in rural districts. The wireless communication standard LTE reaches 92 percent of households. ∎

◻ PANORAMA
A VALUED TRADING PARTNER

Key exports by type of goods (2014)

17.9 %
Cars & automotive
components

14.5 %
Mechanical
equipment

9.5 %
Chemical
products

7.9 %
ICT equipment

6.0 %
Electrical
equipment

Germany's exports (goods)
by region (2014)

European countries make up Germany's main export market, accounting for 68 percent of German exports. They are followed by the USA, which absorbs 8.5 percent, and China with 6.6 percent.

Eurozone
36.6 %

EU excl. the
Eurozone
21.4 %

Rest of
Europe
excl. EU
10.0 %

Australia
Oceania
0.8 %

Africa
2.0 %

1,119 billion euros
Total value of
exported goods

889 billion euros
Value of
imported goods

50 %
of goods are exported

25 %
of jobs depend
on exports

The 25 largest export markets in percent (2014)

United Kingdom: 7.4

USA: 8.5

Sweden: 4.2

Russian Federation: 2.6

Denmark: 1.5

Poland: 4.2

Republic of Korea: 1.4

Mexico: 0.8

Belgium: 3.7

Czech Republic: 3.0

People's Republic of China: 6.6

Brazil: 0.9

Netherlands: 6.5

Germany

Slovakia: 1.0

Turkey: 1.7

Japan: 1.5

Hungary: 1.8

France: 9.0

Romania: 0.9

India: 0.8

Austria: 5.0

United Arab Emirates: 1.0

Spain: 3.1

Switzerland: 4.1

Italy: 4.8

Americas excl. USA 3.5 %

USA 8.5 %

Asia excl. China 10.3 %

China 6.6 %

5.6 million
Cars produced by German manufacturers (in Germany)

9.3 million
Cars produced world-wide by German manufacturers (outside Germany)

150
Key trade fairs in Germany

254
Participations in foreign trade fairs

TOPIC
ATTRACTIVE LABOUR MARKET

Despite the financial and economic crisis, since 2008 the German labour market has tended ever upwards. In July 2015 42.8 million people worked in jobs that are subject to mandatory social insurance contributions. The high employment rate of over 73.5 percent is an expression of the country's sound economic situation, despite little assistance from the global economy. Germany is one of the EU member states with the lowest unemployment. In 2014 the unemployment rate was on average 6.7 percent, and thus at its lowest level since 1991. In particular growth in segments of the services sector is impacting positively on the labour market. According to a study by the Institute for Employment Research (IAB), Germany is set to increasingly become a service society in coming years.

ⓘ INFO

Career Compass Germany.
Created in 2015, the app provides extensive information in German and English about opportunities for training, studying and working in Germany. The app is aimed specifically at young people abroad and gives them an opportunity to familiarise themselves in-depth with all manner of issues. Topics such as corporate culture in German companies as well as helpful guidance with applications are included. There are more than 200 links to associated sites.
→ **deutschland.de**

The rise in part-time employment likewise typically reflects trends in the labour market.

The low level of youth unemployment has drawn the world's attention to the success of dual vocational training, which differs from purely school education. In most countries, the completion of schooling marks the start of working life. Having finished school, almost half of young people in Germany, however, embark on a course of training. These are offered in one of the 350 state-recognised occupations for which accredited vocational training is required within the framework of the dual system. The young people thus receive practical training in their company on three to four weekdays, while on the other day(s) they receive theoretical instruction at a vocational school. Several countries are currently adapting the system of dual vocational training.

With a view to creating a modern, fair and transparent labour market, the Federal Government has moreover realised numerous projects relating to labour-market policy. Since the beginning of 2015, for example, a statutory minimum wage of 8.50 euros has been in place, from which initially 3.7 million people are benefiting. Moreover, the quota for women is intended to ensure equal numbers of men and women in top management positions. This means that from 2016, listed companies and those that are subject to co-determination regulations must adhere to a 30-percent quota for women for

Dual vocational training: the German model, which combines theory and practice, is being adapted in many countries

seats on the supervisory board. Furthermore, the "Collective Bargaining Act" guarantees that within a company different collective wage agreements do not apply for the same work. What is more, as of 1 July 2014 those who can prove that they have paid social security contributions for 45 years can retire without any deductions at the age of 63.

In light of Germany's demographic change, one of the country's most pressing tasks is to secure its skilled labour base. "Make it in Germany", a multi-language Internet portal for international skilled workers, is a major project designed to open up the labour market. It provides information about career opportunities for those interested in coming to Germany and has current job listings for professions in demand (healthcare, engineering and IT). Furthermore, thanks to the EU Blue Card graduates and skilled workers have easy access to the German labour market. ■

ENVIRONMENT & CLIMATE

A Pioneer in Climate Policy • Innovative Force behind Climate Cooperation •
Energy Reform - A Project for Generations •
Greentech – A Sector with a Future • Essential Diversity

INSIGHT

A PIONEER IN CLIMATE POLICY

The 21st century is regarded as the "century of the environment". In other words: the extent to which the natural living conditions of future generations on Earth change will be decided in the next decades. A rise in the speed of climate change is primarily regarded as the main danger. Environmental and climate protection have long been a high priority in Germany. Internationally, Germany leads the way in climate protection and is a pioneer in the development of renewable energy sources.

With the changes to the energy sector, referred to as the Energy Reform, Germany is leaving the age of fossil and nuclear energy clearly behind it and heading fast for a future that hinges on sustainable energy sources. This involves a gradual exit from nuclear power by 2022. Furthermore, by 2020 Germany plans to have reduced its emission of carbon dioxide by 40 percent in comparison to the 1990 levels, and is

even striving for at least 80 percent by 2050. By the end of 2014 it had already achieved a reduction of 27 percent.

Internationally as well, the Federal Government actively supports environmental protection, cooperation on energy issues, and climate-friendly development. Germany is the driving force in the EU, which since the 1992 United Nations summit in Rio de Janeiro has been a pioneer in international climate policy. It supports the objective of limiting global warming to a maximum of two degrees Celsius. To this end, the emission of carbon dioxide in the industrialised countries needs to be reduced by 80 to 95 percent. During Germany's Presidency of the G7 in 2015, the leading industrialised nations resolved to speed up termination of the use of fossil fuels as an energy source. Complete "decarbonisation" is intended to be achieved before the century is out. The UN Secretariat ▶

VIDEO ◼ AR APP

Environment & Climate: the video on the
topic → **tued.net/en/vid4**

There is no turning back on the road to the age of renewable energy

▶ that monitors the implementation of the framework climate convention is based in the Federal City Bonn.

An intact environment – pure air, clean water, varied nature – is a prerequisite for a high quality of life. Since 1994, environmental protection has been a national objective enshrined in the Basic Law. With regard to air and water quality, indicators have for years now evidenced considerable improvement. There has been a sharp fall in the emission of pollutants such as sulphur dioxide and nitrogen oxides – thanks as well to the introduction of filters in coal-fired power stations and catalytic converters in cars. There has also been a noticeable drop in the per capita consumption of drinking water – from a peak of 140 to around 120 litres a day.

Germany is pursuing a strategy of combining economic growth and environmental protection with a view to sustainable economics. In addition to the development of renewable energies, the main contributory factors to this are an increase in the efficient use of energy and resources, and the smart use of regenerative raw materials. It a strategy that pays off twofold, because on the one hand the impact on the environment and climate declines, while on the other new fields of business and jobs are created. ∎

⇒ **INTERNET**

UNFCCC
Secretariat of the United Nations Framework Convention on Climate Change
→ **unfccc.int**

BMUB
Federal Ministry for the Environment, Nature Conservation, Building and Nuclear Safety → **bmub.bund.de**

BUND
Bund für Umwelt- und Naturschutz Deutschland/Friends of the Earth Germany → **bund.net**

In Germany, wind power and solar energy are the most important and inexpensive renewable sources of energy

PLAYERS & ORGANISATIONS

Umweltbundesamt

This authority, which is subordinate to the Federal Ministry for the Environment, provides the Federal Government with scientific expertise. The Umweltbundesamt (Federal Environment Agency) is responsible for enforcing environmental laws, for example the marketing approval of chemicals, medication, and pesticides, as well as informing the public about environmental protection.

→ umweltbundesamt.de

German Energy Agency

The German Energy Agency (DENA) is a centre of expertise for energy efficiency, renewable energy sources, and intelligent energy systems. It supports the implementation of the Energy Reform and promotes the generation and use of energy in as efficient, safe, cost-effective, and environmentally friendly a way as possible.

→ dena.de

Agora Energiewende

The Agora Energiewende think tank sees itself as a forum for dialogue with key stakeholders in the energy policy debate.

→ agora-energiewende.org

Potsdam Institute for Climate Impact Research

This institute addresses key scientific issues relating to global climate change and sustainable development.

→ pik-potsdam.de

Deutsche Gesellschaft für Internationale Zusammenarbeit

Deutsche Gesellschaft für Internationale Zusammenarbeit (GIZ) is a federal enterprise with worldwide operations. It assists the Federal Government in achieving objectives in the field of development. It advises developing and emerging countries on questions relating to environmental protection, as well as on the just and sustainable use of water as a resource.

→ giz.de

Federal Agency for Nature Conservation

The Federal Agency for Nature Conservation (BfN) is responsible for the national and international conservation of nature. Its website features excellent maps of conservation areas.

→ bfn.de

➕ DIGITAL PLUS

More information about all the topics in the chapter – annotated link lists, articles, documents, speeches; plus associated terms such as the Framework Convention on Climate Change, greenhouse gas emissions, the Renewable Energy Sources Act, and EU climate protection objectives.

→ tued.net/en/dig4

TOPIC
INNOVATIVE FORCE BEHIND CLIMATE COOPERATION

Internationally, Germany has played a pivotal role in putting climate protection on the map. The Federal Government was an innovative force as long ago as the negotions leading up to the 1997 Kyoto Protocol. In the treaty, the industrial nations committed to reducing their greenhouse gas emissions by 2012 by an average of 5.2 percent in comparison with the 1990 baseline. Germany actually did much more than that, as it succeeded in lowering emissions by 21 percent by 2012. Germany also plays an active part in the negotiations for a follow-up treaty to the Kyoto Protocol set to come into force in 2020. The goal: a binding climate agreement with clear rules for limiting greenhouse gas emissions. It will involve emerging markets and the Global South also committing to climate protection measures, and will make certain there is a considerable increase in funds for climate adaptation and technology transfer. In the Global North, the EU is a pioneer with regard to carbon dioxide targets; it has pledged to lower emissions by 2030 by at least 40 percent compared with 1990. The main tool is the EU emission trading scheme, which regulates the emission of carbon dioxide by around 11,000 major industrial corporations and power plant operators. It will be reformed with a view to making it more effective. Germany is also actively advancing climate cooperation with other countries, for example as regards issues such as tropical forest protection and energy efficiency.

The "Transatlantic Climate Bridge" represents a particular form of cooperation with the USA and Canada. Germany's pioneering role in climate research is supported by work at universities and institutes such as the Potsdam Institute for Climate Impact Research and the Wuppertal Institute for Climate, Environment and Energy. ∎

MILESTONES

1976
The then German Ministry of Research resolves to build a 100-metre-high large wind power plant (Growian) in north Germany. However, the first experiment with wind power fails and Growian is torn down in 1988.

1987
At Kaiser Wilhelm Koog on the west coast of Schleswig - Holstein, the first German windfarm goes turnkey. Since then, 32 wind turbines have been transforming North Sea wind into electrical power.

1991
The Electricity Feed-In Act regulates the obligation for power utilities to purchase electrical energy from regenerative transformation processes and sets fixed tariffs for the remuneration thereof.

The United Nations' Climate Secretariat in Bonn monitors the Framework Convention on Climate Change

2000

The Renewable Energy Sources Act (EEG) comes into force. Among other things, it lays the legal basis for prioritising renewable sources when feeding electricity into the national grid.

2011

After the nuclear reactor disaster in Fukushima the German Federal cabinet adopts parameters for energy policy: the exit from nuclear power is to be achieved step by step by 2022 and energy supplies placed on an eco-friendly footing.

2014

With the reform of the EEG, the focus turns to cost efficiency and planned feasibility in expanding renewable energy sources; the proportion of eco-electricity in the power mix is set at 40-45 percent by 2025.

TOPIC

ENERGY REFORM – A PROJECT FOR GENERATIONS

The Energy Reform is the single most important economic and environmental policy task in Germany. The Energy Reform refers to the restructuring of the country's energy supply sources away from fossil fuels and nuclear power, towards renewable energies. By 2050 at the latest, a minimum of 80 percent of electricity and 60 percent of all energy in Germany will come from renewable energies, so the plan. The next step will involve gradually shutting down all nuclear power stations by 2022; furthermore, by 2025 40 to 45 percent of electricity will be generated by renewable sources. Since mid-2015 there have only been eight nuclear power stations still in operation, providing around 15 percent of the electricity mix. The Federal Gov-

ernment is thus pressing ahead with the sustainable restructuring of the energy system, which began as long ago as 2000 with the first resolution on an exit from nuclear power and the promotion of the Renewable Energy Sources Act. In Germany the promotion of renewable energies began back in the 1990s and in the year 2000 was made into law in the form of the Renewable Energy Sources Act.

Exit from nuclear power based on long-term planning

Likewise in the year 2000, the Federal Government agreed with the German energy companies on an exit from nuclear power by 2022. As such, the resolutions the Federal Government passed in 2011 follow in the tradition of restructuring of the energy system to rely on sustainable energy sources. It views the accelerated reorganisation of the energy system, which in 2011 the parties represented in the German Bundestag passed with the express approval of a large majority of the population following the nuclear disaster in Fukushima in Japan, as "a necessary step on the way to an industrial society committed to the idea of sustainability and the preservation of Creation".

However, it is not only the environment and climate that are intended to benefit from the Energy Reform, but the German economy as well – the primary aim being to eliminate

≡ LIST

- Largest onshore wind farm:
  Reussenköge in Schleswig-Holstein

- Largest offshore wind farm:
  alpha ventus in the North Sea

- Most powerful wind turbine:
  E126/7570 kW by Enercon

- Largest solar park: **Meuro/Schipkau**

- Biggest electricity exchange: **EEX (European Energy Exchange) in Leipzig**

Offshore wind farms in the North Sea are the main pillars of the Energy Reform

reliance on international imports of crude oil and natural gas. To date, Germany spends around 80 billion euros annually on the import of coal, oil, and gas. In coming years, this amount will be gradually eliminated by domestic value added in the field of renewable energies; moreover, these measures result in additional export opportunities and the prospect of more jobs. Strengthening the "second pillar" of the Energy Reform – the more economical, more efficient use of energy – is another major task. Industry and large business enterprises have already achieved significant savings, and standards are high. Small companies and public facilities still have some catching up to do. Improving the energy consumption of old buildings in particular is especially important with regard to increasing energy efficiency, and the Federal Government makes grants available for the purpose. Buildings account for around 40 percent of carbon dioxide emissions. ▶

▶ Although down slightly since 2007, electricity consumption also needs to be reduced: further efforts are needed to reach the goal of a 10-percent reduction by 2020 outlined in the original energy concept.

The Energy Reform seeks not only to minimise risks, but also to enhance climate-compatible energy consumption and high supply security. The dynamic development of renewable energies has meant an increase in the proportion of carbon dioxide-free energy in the electricity mix. In 2014, green electricity had a 26 percent share of gross electricity generation, and in the first six months of 2015 it accounted for 32.5 percent of total electricity consumption. On sunny work days, solar PV plants can cover up to 25 percent of electricity demand, and on Sundays and public holidays even as much as half. Moreover, 38.7 percent of all new residential buildings are already heated with renewable energies. In early 2015, there were 1.5 million solar PV systems installed, generating approx. 38.5 gigawatts in rated power, putting

Germany in third place behind China and the USA in terms of nameplate capacity.

The Renewable Energy Sources Act an international benchmark

Regarded in several countries as a benchmark, the Renewable Energy Sources Act (EEG) was amended in 2014. The aim was to ensure that the population and business could afford energy, and that its supply was guaranteed. The background: As a result of the strong increase in the number of solar power systems and a different method of calculation, after 2009 there was a considerable increase in what is known as the EEG cost levy, whereby the increased cost of expanding green electricity is passed on to consumers on a pro-rated basis. This sparked a public debate on the cost of green electricity and the Energy Reform. A fall in this share in the costs was seen in 2015 for the first time. The Federal Government is also working on re-designing the structure of the electricity market to ensure stable supplies despite a

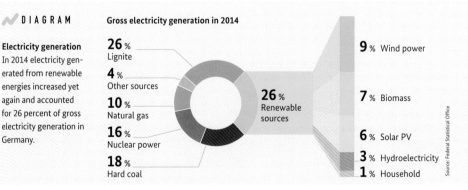

◢ DIAGRAM

Gross electricity generation in 2014

Electricity generation
In 2014 electricity generated from renewable energies increased yet again and accounted for 26 percent of gross electricity generation in Germany.

26 % Lignite

4 % Other sources

10 % Natural gas

16 % Nuclear power

18 % Hard coal

26 % Renewable sources

9 % Wind power

7 % Biomass

6 % Solar PV

3 % Hydroelectricity

1 % Household

Source: Federal Statistical Office

strong increase in the volume of fluctuating wind and solar power generated. Among other things it is about ensuring the availability of gas-fired power stations, which can be used as required, and which emit considerably less carbon dioxide than coal-fired power stations.

The Energy Reform requires not only the establishment of new, "green" power stations. To ensure a reliable supply, power grids have to be adapted to the new structure. To this end there are plans, for example, to add several thousand kilometres of high-voltage lines. This way electricity from wind power, which is primarily enerated in north Germany, can reach the strong economic hubs that are the centres of consumption in the south.

In order to be able to accommodate the solar power that is fed into the network from de-central sources, the regional grids also need to be expanded. Not infrequently this expansion of the grid meets with resistance on the part of the residents in regions in which the

new routes will run close to residential areas. The grid operators attempt to take concerns into consideration at an early stage. So as to defuse conflicts, thought is also being given to laying the electricity cables in underground cables. ∎

GLOBAL

Climate study
800 scientists from 80 countries work for the United Nations' Intergovernmental Panel on Climate Change (IPCC).
In spring 2015, the panel of experts issued the Synthesis Report of the Fifth IPCC Assessment Report. It states that greenhouse gas emissions are the main cause of climate change. Drastic steps are needed if global warming is to be limited to two degrees Celsius.
→ ipcc.ch

Carbon dioxide emissions in 2013/worldwide share

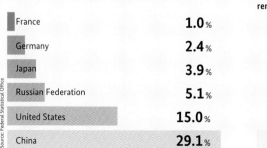

France	**1.0**%
Germany	**2.4**%
Japan	**3.9**%
Russian Federation	**5.1**%
United States	**15.0**%
China	**29.1**%

Source: Federal Statistical Office

Share of electricity in Germany generated from renewable sources (terawatt forecast)

| 2007 | 2014 | 2020 | 2050 |
| **14**% | **28**% | **35**% | **80**% |

Source: Fraunhofer ISE/BDEW/BMWi

TOPIC
GREENTECH – A SECTOR WITH A FUTURE

Both the economy and the labour market are benefitting from the leading role Germany plays in technologies for environmental protection, renewable energies, and the efficient use of resources. The environment sector is making a considerable contribution to sustainable growth and is helping the development of new technologies – in the fields of energy generation, ICT, and materials technology. Around two million people work in the environmental technology sector; almost every fifth job is labelled "green". This puts Germany among the ten leading countries in terms of empl oyment in the various segments of the renewable energy sector.

NUMBER

1.79 million

kilometres is the length of the German national grid. You could circumnavigate the globe at the Equator 45 times using the cables. The vast majority of the grid, namely a total of 1.44 million kilometres or 80 percent, is underground. Around 350,000 kilometres are power lines. The supra-regional high-voltage lines are 34,810 kilometres long. About 2,650 kilometres of new power lines are being planned as part of the Energy Reform.
→ bundesnetzagentur.de

Overall the latter is shaped by small to medium-size enterprises, though corporations such as Siemens are important players. Under the label "GreenTech Made in Germany" the companies are posting considerable export successes; their share of the global market is around 15 percent. With an "Environmental Technology Export Initiative" Germany intends to improve its situation still further and would like to position itself primarily as an integrated solutions provider.

Electromobility will be an important future issue in the environmental sector

Electromobility is also expected to give environmental and climate protection a further boost. The electromobility of the future is likewise a key issue being addressed today in China, Japan, and North America. The Federal Government and the automotive industry are jointly pursuing the ambitious goal of making Germany the leading market for electromobility and locking into the immense potential this global market has to offer. The plan is for there to be around one million electric cars on Germany's roads by 2020, helping lower carbon dioxide emissions still further, a sixth of which stems from road traffic. The German car manufacturers are addressing e-mobility concepts in great depth and have around 29 electric models in their ranges (as at the end of 2015), including vehicles such as the

Electromobility is one of the major topics the German automotive industry will address in the future

BMW i3. In order to help electric cars make their breakthrough, the Federal Government has promised that owners of such vehicles will be allowed to use bus lanes, will enjoy reserved parking spaces, and special registration plates. It has also considerably increased spending on energy research, with a particular focus on more powerful batteries for electric cars. The "2020 Battery" project is regarded as a showcase project and is intended to produce evolutionary, advanced materials for R&D on the most efficient battery systems.

In the meantime German and European universities and higher education institutes now offer around 1,000 innovative courses in the field of renewable energies and energy efficiency, which attract many international students. ∎

PANORAMA
SUSTAINABLE ENERGIES

Inner workings of a modern German wind turbine
Enercon E-126 type with a 4,200 kW power rating

❶ Machine frame
❷ Yaw drive
❸ Ring generator
❹ Blade pitch control
❺ Rotor hub
❻ Rotor blade

Windpower plants
The wind drives the rotor blades. The generator transforms the mechanical energy into electrical power.

Transformer house
The transformer feeds the power at the right voltage to the grid operator.

Substation
The substation transforms the medium voltage into high voltage for transmission over greater distances.

690 V

10,000 V – 30,000 V

110,000 V

50 %
more electricity from renewable sources

30 %
less electricity from nuclear power stations

371,000
employees in the renewable energy sector

18,000
new jobs p.a. thanks to the Energy Reform (through 2020)

Use of windpower and solar energy by federal state
in output (MW)

- ⚪ Solar energy
- ⚫ Wind power

32.5 %
In first-half 2015, 32.5 percent of the electrical energy consumed was generated by renewable sources.

....

25,000
At year-end 2014 a total of 25,000 wind-power plants were installed in Germany.

....

1.5 million
At year-end 2014 1.5 million solar PV plants were installed in Germany.

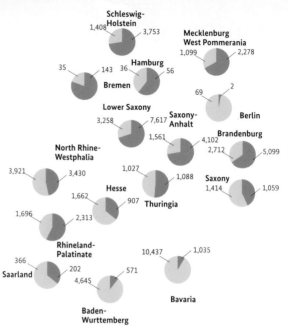

Schleswig-Holstein 1,408 / 3,753

Mecklenburg West Pommerania 1,099 / 2,278

Hamburg 36 / 56

Bremen 35 / 143

Lower Saxony 3,258 / 7,617

Saxony-Anhalt 1,561 / 4,102

Berlin 69 / 2

Brandenburg 2,712 / 5,099

North Rhine-Westphalia 3,921 / 3,430

Hesse 1,027 / 1,088

Saxony 1,414 / 1,059

Thuringia 1,662 / 907

Rhineland-Palatinate 1,696 / 2,313

Saarland 366 / 202

Baden-Wurttemberg 4,645 / 571

Bavaria 10,437 / 1,035

Power grid
Electricity is distributed to the individual regions via the high-voltage power grid.

Substation
In a second substation the high voltage is stepped down to 230 volts.

Households
A 5 MW windpower plant can supply electricity to some 4,900 households a year – and to about 14,600 persons.

Up to 380,000V

230V

12.3 billion euros
for new windpower plants (2014)

3.1 billion euros
for new solar-power plants (2014)

1.79
million kilometres of cable for the power grid

35,000
kilometres of "power highways"

TOPIC
ESSENTIAL DIVERSITY

Germany is a country with great biological diversity. Around 48,000 animal species, and 24,000 types of higher plants, mosses, fungi, lichens, and algae are native to the country. Having been enshrined in the Basic Law in 1994, the protection of the natural habitats is an official goal of government. Between the North Sea and the Alps, the lawmakers have designates 16 national parks and 15 UNESCO biosphere reserves that are totally different in character, along with thousands of nature reserves.

Germany is a signatory state to the most important international agreements on biodiversity, and a party to around 30 intergovernmental treaties and programmes with nature protection as their goal. By ratifying the United Nations' Convention on Biodiversity, the governments of 196 countries pledged to significantly reduce the rate of loss of biological diversity. To date, however, no turnaround in the extinction of species has been achieved. In 2010, an international framework for access to genetic resources and just benefit sharing was passed at the Conference of Parties to the Convention in Nagoya (Japan). The Nagoya Protocol has been in force since 2014.

In Germany more than 40 percent of vertebrates and plant species are considered to be endangered. For this reason, efforts aimed at nature conservation and species protection on land, in the water, and in the North and Baltic Seas are to be stepped up. The primary objective is to reduce the destruction of habitats by house and road building, as well as the pollution levels that result, among other things, from intensive farming and over-fertilisation. The amount of land used for housing construction and new transport routes is intended to be reduced from 70 to 30 hectares daily. A further aim is to allow "wilderness" on two percent of the nation's territory and give five percent of forests over to nature. In 2015, numerous former military zones covering a total of 31,000 hectares, including moors and heaths, were devoted to nature conservation.

ⓘ INFO

Wild animals For several years now, an increasing number of wild animals have been resettling in Germany. In more than 30 packs, an estimated total of 300 wolves are now roaming the eastern and northern federal states. Wild cats and lynxes are being sighted ever more frequently. The number of pairs of breeding sea eagles has reached unprecedented heights; otters are almost a familiar sight again. There have even been occasional sightings of elks and brown bears, which are wandering into Germany from neighbouring countries in the east.
→ wwf.de

UNESCO biosphere reserves and national parks in Germany

Wadden Sea mudflats and Hallig
islands of Schleswig-Holstein
Hamburg mudflats
Lower Saxon mudflats

Western Pomeranian
Boddenlandschaft
Jasmund
Southeast Rügen

Lake Schaalsee
Müritz
Lower Oder Valley
Elbe River Landscape
Schorfheide-Chorin

Spree Forest
Harz
Upper Lusatian
Moorland
South Harz Karst
Landscape
Kellerwald-Edersee
Hainich
Saxon Switzerland
Eifel
Rhön
Vessertal-
Thuringian Forest
Hunsrück-Hochwald
Bliesgau
Palatinate Forest-North Vosges
Bavarian Forest
Black Forest
Swabian Alb

National Park
Land Biosphere Reserve

Berchtesgadener Land
Berchtesgaden

Increasing attention is being paid to the protection of the marine environment. Seas are rich in biological diversity, and a source of raw materials, energy, and food. The ecosystem is highly contaminated through oil production, shipping, over-fishing, the influx of poorly degradable substances (plastic waste) and acidification through carbon dioxide. Data compiled by the UN Food and Agriculture Organization (FAO) reveal that global fish and aquaculture production has more than doubled since the 1980s. At the 2015 G7 Summit in Elmau the heads of state and government discussed ways of better preserving the maritime ecosystem. In future living wild animals from Asia, Africa, and Latin America that have been caught in the wild and are offered for sale on the German market will also be afforded greater protection. The import into the EU of animals caught in the wild as well as commercial wild animal exchanges in Germany are to be banned. ∎

EDUCATION & KNOWLEDGE

Vibrant Hub of Knowledge • Dynamic Academic Landscape •
Ambitious Cutting-edge Research • Networking Academia • Research and Academic
Relations Policy • Excellent Research • Attractive School System

INSIGHT

VIBRANT HUB OF KNOWLEDGE

Germany is one of the top places in the world for research and academic training. This is symbolised by the fact that with more than 80 awards, Germany places third among the nations with the most Nobel laureates. In a globalised world in which knowledge is regarded as the most important resource, the country, with its long-standing tradition of research and development, is well positioned in the international competition for the best minds. Three major aspects shape this vibrant hub of knowledge: the dense network of around 400 higher education institutions, the four internationally renowned non-university research organisations, and strong industrial research. The country has its impressive research achievements to thank for the fact that with 12 percent of global trade volume, Germany is the world's leading exporter of high-tech goods and in the European Union (EU) is assured a firm place in the group of innovation leaders. Internationally, Germany is in the top group of those few countries to invest more than 2.5 percent of their gross domestic product in research and development.

With numerous measures and reforms, the government and higher education institutions took the initiative to advance Germany as a hub of knowledge and place it on a more international footing. The Qualification Initiative adopted in 2008 offers lifelong training programmes, formed part of this. Other success stories include the Excellence Initiative, which has spawned a number of internationally oriented graduate schools and clusters of excellence, the Higher Education Pact 2020, the High-Tech Strategy, the Research and Innovation Pact, and the Strategy for the Internationalisation of Science and Research. As Europe's biggest research nation, in 2014 Germany was the first EU Mem- ▶

VIDEO ◯◀ AR APP

Education & Knowledge: the video on
the topic → **tued.net/en/vid5**

As a place to study, Germany is one of the most popular destinations for international students

▶ ber State to formulate a strategy for further shaping the European Research Area (ERA).

Particular attention is paid to an international focus. As part of the Bologna Process, most higher education courses now lead to Bachelor's and Master's degrees, with many of them offered in a foreign language. For international students Germany is already the most popular country to study in after the USA and Great Britain. At 30 percent, the proportion of students from Germany who spend time studying abroad is high. The number of international members of staff at higher education institutions also rose by about two thirds in the last decade, and stands at 10 percent. Many German higher education institutions are involved in the "export" of degree courses and the establishment of higher education institutions based on the German model in the international education market. In comparison with other countries, the German education system is in principle relatively well adapted to the needs of the labour market. 86 percent of adults in Germany have a university entrance qualification or successfully completed vocational training. The OECD average is only 75 percent. ■

➡ **INTERNET**

Research Explorer
A research directory containing more than 23,000 institutes
→ research-explorer.de

Research in Germany
Major information platform about Germany as a centre of innovation
→ research-in-germany.org

DWIH
German Houses of Research and Innovation worldwide
→ germaninnovation.info

Stepping-stone to a successful career: a university degree

PLAYERS & ORGANISATIONS

German Research Foundation
The German Research Foundation (DFG) is the main organisation for funding research at higher education and publicly financed institutes.
→ **dfg.de**

German Rectors' Conference
The German Rectors' Conference (HRK) is a voluntary association of state and state-recognised higher education institutions in Germany. The Higher Education Compass database provides information about degree courses and international cooperation agreements.
→ **hrk.de, hochschulkompass.de**

Leopoldina
The oldest academy of sciences in the world, the Leopoldina in Halle, has 1,500 members.
→ **leopoldina.org**

Non-university research organisations
The Max Planck Society, the Fraunhofer Gesellschaft, the Helmholtz Association and the Leibniz Association are the non-university research organisations funded by the Federal Government and the states.
→ **mpg.de, fraunhofer.de, helmholtz.de, leibniz-gemeinschaft.de**

Alexander von Humboldt Foundation
The Humboldt Foundation supports cutting-edge scientists and scientific exchange.
→ **humboldt-foundation.de**

German Academic Exchange Service
The German Academic Exchange Service (DAAD) is the largest funding organisation for exchanges of students and academics. It has a global network with 71 regional offices and information centres.
→ **daad.de, studieren-in.de**

Alumniportal Deutschland
The Alumniportal Deutschland networks people who have studied, done research or worked in Germany all over the world.
→ **alumniportal-deutschland.org**

"Schools: Partners for the Future" initiative
The Federal Foreign Office initiative links almost 2,000 schools all over the world at which German is held in high esteem.
→ **pasch-net.de**

➕ DIGITAL PLUS
More information about all the topics in the chapter – annotated link lists, articles, documents, speeches; plus more in-depth information about key topics such as the Bologna Process, internationalisation, degrees, admissions restriction.
→ **tued.net/en/dig5**

TOPIC

DYNAMIC ACADEMIC LANDSCAPE

The German academic landscape is highly diverse: There are famous universities in major cities such as Berlin and Munich, along with excellent higher education institutions in Aachen, Heidelberg, and Karlsruhe. Medium-sized universities with a strong focus on research and smaller colleges with an outstanding reputation form the nucleus of the academic world. Whether the international Shanghai Ranking, the QS World University Rankings, or the Times Higher Education World University Rankings – each lists between 10 and 12 German universities among the Top 200. Munich's Ludwig-Maximilians-Universität, Heidelberg University and Technische Universität München (TUM) do particularly well.

≣ LIST

• Oldest university: **Heidelberg University (founded in 1386)**

• Youngest university: **Medizinische Hochschule Brandenburg (founded in 2014)**

• Biggest university: **Ludwig-Maximilians-Universität München (50,327 students)**

• Most attractive university for international cutting-edge and young academics: **Freie Universität Berlin (2014 Humboldt Ranking)**

According to the German Rectors' Conference (HRK), in 2015 students in Germany could choose between 399 higher education institutions (121 universities, 220 universities of applied sciences, and 58 art and music academies). Together they offer 17,731 courses. As part of the Bologna Process to create a uniform European Higher Education Area (EHEA) initiated in 1999, 87.4 percent of all courses now lead to Bachelor's and Master's degrees. 238 higher education institutions are funded by the state, 40 by the church, and 121 privately.

Most popular non-English-speaking host country for international students

In terms of structure and purpose, the higher education landscape is basically divided up threefold. We distinguish between universities, universities of applied sciences and academies of art, film and music. Whereas the classic universities offer a wide range of subjects, the technical universities (TU) concentrate on basic research in engineering and natural science disciplines. In 2006 the nine leading technical universities formed the TU9 Initiative. The universities regard themselves not only as teaching institutes but as research centres too, and as such even today embody Wilhelm von Humboldt's educational ideal of the unity of research and teaching. The universities' primary objective is to promote young academics, pass on substantiated spe-

There are 2.7 million students enrolled at around 400 higher education institutions in Germany

cialist knowledge, and train academics to work and research independently. The 220 strongly practice-oriented universities of applied sciences (FH) are unique to Germany. The introduction of the right of universities of applied sciences to award doctorates, which at present only universities are allowed to do, is currently under discussion.

Overall, the number of people engaged in academic pursuits is increasing: Whereas in 2005 the ratio of freshmen stood at 37 percent, around half of young people in Germany now take up higher education. The Federal Training Assistance Act (BAföG) enables them to complete a degree course independently of their family's financial situation. Nonetheless, educational success remains closely linked to social background – only 23 percent of children from non-academic households embark on a degree. In 2014 there were 2.7 million students registered at higher ▶

MAP
Clusters of excellence, graduate schools and Excellence Initiative institutional strategies

Legend:

- ■ Institutional strategy
- ▨ Graduate school
- ▦ Cluster of excellence
- ◪ Co-applicants

- U University
- TU Technical University
- HU Humboldt-Universität
- LU Leibniz-Universität
- JU Jacobs University
- FU Freie Universität
- LMU Ludwig-Maximilians-Univ.
- MedH Medical school

education institutions, among them 301,350 with a non-German passport: 218,848 students who gained their university entrance qualification abroad and 82,502 foreigners with a German entrance qualification (Abitur).

Since 2011 the total number of students has risen by 18 percent, the number of international students by almost 20 percent in the same period. Today there are twice as many foreigners enrolled at German universities as in 1996. Most international students come from China, Russia, and India. This makes Germany the most popular non-Eng-

lish-speaking host country for international students. Only the USA and Great Britain are more attractive. The technical universities have a particularly good reputation for training engineers – 25 percent of freshmen there are international students.

At the same time the German higher education institutions have increased the number of foreign-language and international courses to 1,104. The multitude of structured doctoral courses is particularly attractive for international doctoral students. The fact that for the most part most German higher education institutions do not charge tuition fees gives them a further advantage.

The Federal Government and the states are tackling the increasing numbers engaged in academic study together: In late 2014, as part of the Higher Education Pact 2020, they resolved to finance up to 760,000 additional university entrants in the coming years. For the entire duration of the Higher Education Pact from 2007 to 2023, the Federal Government will provide 20.2 billion euros, and the states 18.3 billion euros.

Initiatives for more excellence and greater internationalisation

Since 2005 the Federal Government and the states have been funding particularly outstanding research projects and facilities through the Excellence Initiative. In the current stage of the programme (2012–2017) 45 graduate schools, 43 clusters of excellence and 11 institutional strategies spread across 44 universities are receiving funding. The volume of funding in this period totals 2.7 billion euros. A similar level of funding is intended after 2017 as well.

Internationalisation remains an important topic. A 2014 joint study by the German Academic Exchange Service (DAAD), the German Rectors' Conference, and the Humboldt Foundation identified around 31,000 international cooperation agreements concluded by almost 300 higher education institutions with 5,000 higher education partners in 150 countries, among them many programmes leading to double degrees. Many higher education institutions are involved in the development of German study courses and the founding of higher education institutions based on the German model, which exist in Egypt, China, Jordan, Kazakhstan, Mongolia, Oman, Singapore, Hungary, Vietnam, and Turkey.

Increasing foreign mobility among German students is likewise being funded. Among 30 percent already spend time studying abroad. In future it is intended that every second German graduate of a higher education institution gain experience abroad while studying. Scholarships such as the Erasmus+ programme support these valuable study visits.   ∎

⊙ I N F O

Programme for Women Professors
Women in Germany are nowadays more likely than men to study, and write almost half of all doctoral theses – but only 21.3 percent of professors are female. This is why in 2008 the Federal Government and the states launched the Programme for Women Professors. With a budget of 300 million euros up until 2017, the programme is designed to increase the number of women professors and promote equality. May 2015 saw the appointment of the 400th woman professor whose position is funded by the programme.
→ bmbf.de/de/494.php

TOPIC
AMBITIOUS CUTTING-EDGE RESEARCH

Science and research are held in high esteem in Germany. Over the past few years, businesses and the government have continually increased their knowledge work budgets. In 2013 the proportion of the gross domestic product (GDP) spent on research was 2.84 percent. Internationally this put Germany in the top group of countries that invest more than 2.5 percent of their GDP in research and development (R&D). In 2013 in Germany a total of almost 80 billion euros was spent on R&D. Industry accounts for around 67 percent of spending on research, with higher education institutions contributing 18 percent and the state 15 percent. The European Commission's "Innovation Union Scoreboard 2015" study places Germany, together with Sweden, Denmark and Finland, in the top group of "innovation leaders" in the European Union (EU). On a worldwide level, Germany accounts for seven percent of global spending on R&D, even though it only has 1.2 percent of the world's population. Between 2010 and 2013, industrial companies in Germany increased spending on R&D by more than 22 percent to in excess of 57 billion euros, thus investing more than ever in innovation. Between 2005 and 2015 the Federal Government increased its spending on education and research by 65 percent. In 2015, 15.3 billion euros are earmarked for the education and research budget, with further growth of 25 percent envisaged by 2017.

German academics' results are highly presentable: In the Nature Index Global, which evaluates the publication output of research facilities and higher education institutions, published in late 2014, Germany achieved top marks in Europe. At the international level it is in third place behind the USA and China. ▶

✔ DIAGRAM

Germany – a high-tech location
604,600 men and women work in research and development in Germany; 360,900 of them are researchers. In terms of human resources and spending, the sectors with the greatest focus on research are pharmaceuticals, aerospace, and automotive construction.

Patents of relevance to global markets in EU countries, per million inhabitants

Sweden	**464**
Finland	**459**
Germany	**370**
Denmark	**328**
⋮	
EU average	**153**

Source: BMBF/Federal Report on Research and Innovation

Never before has investment in research and development been as high as it is today

R&D – human resources by sector

Source: OECD/BMBF/Federal Statistical Office

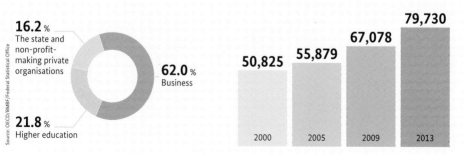

16.2% The state and non-profit-making private organisations

62.0% Business

21.8% Higher education

Spending on research and development in million €

50,825 — 2000
55,879 — 2005
67,078 — 2009
79,730 — 2013

▶ **Since 2006 Germany** has developed a particular innovation tool in the form of its interdepartmental High-Tech Strategy. Since then, High-Tech Strategy research projects have prompted a raft of innovations – from energy-saving LED bulbs to a tissue-engineered heart valve. The High-Tech Strategy initially had the market potential of specific fields of technology in its sights, whereas since 2010 it has been focussing on society's need for solutions that are fit for the future, and their realisation.

cutting-edge clusters which receive special funding were selected in three competition rounds. In 2014 an evaluation revealed that the cutting-edge clusters had produced 900 innovative products, 300 patents, 450 dissertation and habilitation theses, 1,000 Bachelor's and Master's theses, and 40 start-ups. Germany boasts more than 800 publicly financed research facilities. Alongside higher education institutions, it is primarily four non-university research organisations that form the backbone of the research sector.

Translating good ideas into innovative products

Excellent non-university research institutions

In 2014 the High-Tech Strategy was redefined: The goal is to help researchers address topics with future potential and swiftly translate good ideas into innovative products. Six thematic priorities serve as orientation: the digital economy and society, the sustainable economy and energy, the innovative workplace, healthy living, intelligent mobility and civil security. Within the framework of the High-Tech Strategy, 15

Founded in 1948, the Max Planck Society (MPG) is the most important centre for conducting basic research outside universities in the natural sciences, life sciences, social sciences, and the humanities. 5,600 researchers, 40 percent of them international scientists, work at the 78 Max Planck Institutes in Germany and five other institutes in the Netherlands, Luxembourg, Italy, and the USA. Since it was established, the Max

---

▯ MILESTONES

1995

At the Fraunhofer Institute in Erlangen, a team headed by electrical engineer and mathematician Karlheinz Brandenburg develops the MP3 procedure for compressing audio data, which is nowadays standard throughout the world.

2005

The Excellence Initiative is announced for higher education institutions. The Joint Initiative for Research and Innovation provides funding for non-university research organisations.

2008

Nine years after the discovery of the giant magnetoresistance effect, which led to the breakthrough of gigabyte hard drives, the German Peter Grünberg and the Frenchman Albert Fert are awarded the Nobel Prize in Physics.

Planck Society has produced 18 Nobel laureates. It is number two and the only European research organisation in the Top 10 in the worldwide ISI Citation Index of the most-quoted research works in 22 fields.

The Helmholtz Association conducts cutting-edge research in six fields: energy, earth and environment, health, aeronautics, space and transport, key technologies and matter. The Helmholtz scientists concentrate on highly complex systems and projects. With 14,700 scientists and 6,200 doctoral students at the 18 independent Helmholtz centres, including the German Aerospace Center (DLR), which has 16 sites alone, it is Germany's biggest research organisation.

With 66 institutes, the Fraunhofer Gesellschaft is considered to be the largest application-oriented development organisation in Europe. Its most important fields of research are health, security, communication, mobility, energy, and the environment. With subsidiaries and offices, not to mention cooperation agreements, in no less than nine European countries, two in each of North and South America, seven Asian, three African and Arab countries, as well as in Australia, it has a truly global research reach.

The Leibniz Association is the umbrella connecting 89 independent research institutions that range in focus from the natural sciences, engineering and environmental sciences through economics, spatial and social sciences to the humanities. A focus common to the 9,200 researchers is knowledge transfer to policy makers, industry, and the general public.

The German Research Foundation (DFG), Europe's largest organisation of this kind, is responsible for funding science and research. Alongside its head office in Bonn, the DFG maintains offices in China, Japan, India, Russia, North and Latin America, and promotes cooperation between researchers in Germany and fellow researchers abroad. ■

2012

The European Patent Office honours Heidelberg physicist Josef Bille, the inventor of the eye laser, for his lifetime achievement. With almost 100 patents, Bille paved the way for present-day eye surgery using lasers.

2014

Stefan Hell, a Director at the Max Planck Institute for Biophysical Chemistry, together with two US researchers receives the Nobel Prize in Chemistry for developing high resolution fluorescence microscopy.

2015

At almost 90 percent, the changeover to two-cycle Bachelor's and Master's degree courses is for the most part complete. State-regulated degree courses, Medicine and Law are an exception.

TOPIC
NETWORKING ACADEMIA

Globalisation is also presenting the German academic landscape with new challenges. The ability to network knowledge and academics plays a major role here. In this respect, Germany has positioned itself well. Almost half of its academic publications are now written by researchers working on international co-operation projects. According to data compiled for the "Wissenschaft Weltoffen 2015" report, which provides facts and figures on the international nature of studies and research in Germany, there were 38,094 academic and artistic members of staff, among them 2,886 professors, working at the 399 higher education institutions – that is 10 percent of all employees. Since 2006 the number of foreign academic staff has risen by 74 percentage points; the number of professors grew by 46 percent. The recently simplified visa procedures for academics from non-EU member states has likewise played a role in promoting this development.

A positive trend can moreover be observed in the number of foreign researchers receiving funding for their stay in Germany. The key countries of origin of those experts 56,310 currently working in the Federal Republic are Russia, China, India, the USA, and Italy. In many cases higher education institutions and research organisations set up welcome centres, so as to be able to give the international academics greater support as they settle in. Temporary stays by researchers are also regarded as beneficial, for having returned to their home countries, they often become important network partners for further collaborations.

Many academics from abroad are attracted to Germany by the country's excellent research infrastructure, which includes the opportunity to work on large-scale research facilities, which in some cases are the only ones of their kind in the world. The Helmholtz Association alone operates some 50 large-scale facilities for a wide range of research fields. Numerous academics from abroad, who are leading in their field, come to German universities on a Humboldt Professorship, Germany's most highly endowed research prize, which is worth five million euros and is awarded by the Humboldt Foundation.

17,686 German academics have received funding to conduct research abroad; the most important sponsors are the German Research Foundation (DFG), the European Marie Curie Fellowship programme, and in particular the German Academic Exchange Service (DAAD), the world's largest funding organisation for student and academic exchange, from which almost two thirds of the students and academics to receive funding were awarded a scholarship.

Germany aims to develop and expand international academic collaboration, while at the same time elevating it to the next level of

At German universities and academic institutes, research in international teams is part of everyday life

quality. The International Cooperation Action Plan approved by the Federal Ministry of Education and Research (BMBF) in 2014 serves as the basis for this.

Ambitious realignment of the internationalisation strategy

On the basis of the action plan, the Strategy for the Internationalisation of Science and Research launched in 2008 will be realigned and adapted to recent changes. This includes developing the European Research Area (ERA) within the European Union, whose consolidation Germany strongly endorses, as it gives researchers the chance to enjoy freedom of movement and academic findings, while technologies will be freely exchanged. The action plan also outlines the shape of future cooperation agreements with developing and emerging nations and explains how Germany can play a major role in solving global challenges. ■

TOPIC
RESEARCH AND ACADEMIC RELATIONS POLICY

Academic exchange is a pillar of international cultural and educational policy. In its implementation, key partners of the Federal Foreign Office are the German Academic Exchange Service (DAAD), the Alexander von Humboldt Foundation, the German Archaeological Institute (DAI) along with the foundations of the political parties with an international focus. In 2009, in his first term of office, Federal Foreign Minister Frank-Walter Steinmeier launched the Research and Academic Relations Initiative. Its aim: to buttress tried-and-tested methods and expand them to include new strategies. It has already inspired countless new ideas in exchange; and consciously supports further networking around the globe.

Worldwide, five German Houses of Research and Innovation (DWIH) in Moscow, New Delhi, New York, São Paulo and Tokyo, as well as the German Science Centre (DWZ) in Cairo promote scientific collaboration with Germany. They regard themselves as showcases for Germany as a research and innovation location, and pool information and the existing structures of German research institutions in these countries. For this reason they are the first point of contact for all academics interested in collaborating with Germany.

Furthermore, since 2010 the German Academic Exchange Service has funded the work of four new Centres of Excellence in Russia, Thailand, Chile, and Columbia: these network hundreds of international scientists with German research and train young academics to the highest standards. In each case they are conceived as collaborations in research and teaching between a German higher education institution and one or several foreign partner institutes.

NUMBER

177 million

euros was the amount the Federal Foreign Office contributed to the budget of the German Academic Exchange Service (DAAD) in 2014. This is the biggest individual item, accounting for 40 percent in total. The funds are used to run a wide range of foreign cultural and education policy projects and programmes.

Academic cooperation with crisis and conflict regions

A major focal point of the research and academic relations policy is cooperation with academics and higher education institutions in crisis and conflict regions, as well as in transition countries. With this complex commitment there are hopes that cooperation in research and higher education can

In 2015 Federal Foreign Minister Steinmeier (in the centre) visited the German-Columbian Centre of Excellence, CEMarin

pave the way for political understanding, and that as such crisis prevention and crisis management can frequently be made possible. Higher education can thus become a basis for sustainable development and provide people with the necessary expertise for self-help by qualifying future decision-makers; and as such impacting directly on society.

One result of the numerous crises and conflicts the world has seen in the most recent past is that young people are being denied education. For this reason, in 2014 the Federal Foreign Office, together with the German Academic Exchange Service, launched the "Leadership for Syria" programme, which enables over 200 Syrian scholarship holders to study in Germany. Following the conflict in the Balkans, much has been achieved with regard to rebuilding aca-

demic structures in southeastern Europe, and since 2002 in Afghanistan, for example through a variety of efforts by German higher education institutions in IT and economics. Academic development work is also underway in central Iraq and Kurdistan Iraq.

Transition partnership with countries in the Arab world

Furthermore, since 2001 Germany has conducted a transition partnership with several Arab countries. The idea is to support reform efforts at Arab universities through cooperation projects with German higher education institutions. Moreover, the numerous "Good Governance" programmes aimed at future leaders in crisis regions worldwide constitute a particularly important field. ∎

◻ PANORAMA
EXCELLENT RESEARCH

Rosetta probe
The probe travelled
through space for
ten years to install
Philae on the Chury-
umov-Gerasimenko
comet.

Rosetta mission
The European Space Agency (ESA) is researching
the history of how our solar system was formed.
The German Aerospace Center (DLR) played a major
role in building the Philae lander and runs the lander
control centre which oversaw the daring landing on
a comet, a task never before accomplished.

Philae lander

Philae lander
Philae was the first
device to soft-land
on a comet.

6 cranes
9 hoists

Weight:	100 kg
Dimension:	1 x 1 x 0.8 m
Landing:	21 November 2014

SCIENCE

Neumayer Station III
In the eternal ice of the Antarctic, the Alfred Wegener
Institute maintains the Neumayer Station III, where
researchers can live and work year-round. It is built on
hydraulic supports and adapts to changes in snow cover.

Mass:	2,300 tons
Size:	68 x 24 m
Usable space:	4,890 m² on four levels
Laboratory/office:	12 rooms
Living quarters:	15 rooms, 40 beds

399
higher education institutes
and universities

2.7 million
students at
higher education institutions

€ 79.7 billion
spent on research
and development

360,900
researchers

Sonne research vessel

Sonne is the most recent addition to the German research fleet and has been probing the secrets of the deep sea since 2014, primarily in the Pacific and in the Indian Ocean. The high-tech ship is regarded as the most modern in the world.

Cabin deck
with 33 cabins for crew members

Communal deck with
mess and library

Work deck
8 labs across 600 m²

Storage deck
with cabins for
20 scientists

Length:	116 m
Speed:	12.5 knots
Max. time at sea:	52 days
Personnel (max.):	40 people
Deployment:	Indian Ocean, Pacific

Multi-corer
It can simultaneously take lots of small samples from the seabed.

Water extractor
This device takes water samples and measures temperature and depth.

Underwater vehicle
It is remote controlled and equipped with a video camera and gripper arms.

83
Max Planck
Institutes worldwide

66
Fraunhofer
Institutes

89
Leibniz Association
research facilities

18
Helmholtz Association
research centres

TOPIC
ATTRACTIVE SCHOOL SYSTEM

In Germany responsibility for the school system is primarily with the 16 federal states. This is why there are different education systems and plans, along with different types of school. The Standing Conference of the Ministers of Education and Cultural Affairs of the Länder in the Federal Republic of Germany (KMK) guarantees the conformity or comparability of the education programmes and the certificates awarded. In the 2014-5 academic year there were almost 11 million pupils attending 44,880 general-education and vocational schools, with 795,600 teachers giving instruction. Furthermore there are some 969,000 pupils enrolled at 6,620 private general-education and vocational schools. In general, school attendance is compulsory for all children from the age of six for a nine-year period. At the same time the promotion of early education at pre-school age and its interlocking with primary schooling is a high-priority issue in education policy. 10,000 all-day schools now have a firm place in the education system. It is expected that teaching in these schools will result in an increased level of equal opportunities, especially for children from educationally deprived backgrounds.

Attendance at state schools is free of charge. The school system is divided vertically into three levels: primary education and secondary education levels I and II. As a rule, all children attend a primary school, which lasts from Year 1 to 4 (in Berlin and Brandenburg 1 to 6). Subsequently there are three standard curricula: the secondary general school curriculum (Years 5 to 9 or 10), the intermediate school curriculum (Years 5 to 10, "Mittlere Reife" or middle school diploma) and the grammar school curriculum (Years 5 to 12 or 13, general higher education entrance diploma; or Abitur). These are taught either in separate types of school or in schools which combine two or – as in the case of comprehensive schools – three of the curricula and facilitate switching between the different types of school. The names of these types of school vary depending on the state; only grammar schools (Gymnasium) are known

⊕ **GLOBAL**

PISA survey Published in late 2013, the fifth Programme for International Student Assessment (PISA) comparative survey conducted by the OECD revealed that for the first time schoolchildren in Germany were well above the OECD average in all subjects. Among other things, this success is thanks to the extensive measures taken by the Federal Government and the states to improve education. The next PISA survey will be published in late 2016.

→ oecd.org/pisa

OECD
PISA

Some 8.4 million pupils attend general-education schools

as such in all states. In 2014 432,700 pupils were awarded the higher education entrance diploma entitling them to study at a university or university of applied sciences. For children with special needs there are separate schools which, depending on the particular disability, provide adequate facilities to help them learn and develop. In line with the UN Convention on the Rights of People with Disabilities, children with and without disability being taught together is intended to become the rule.

In 72 countries the 140 German schools abroad provide an excellent education to around 20,800 German and 61,000 non-German pupils. Most are run privately, but are supported by the Central Agency for German Schools Abroad (ZfA). Since 2008 the PASCH initiative, ZfA and Goethe-Institut have been working on forming an even bigger network of German students. Worldwide it links almost 2,000 schools, with more than 600,000 pupils learning German there. ∎

SOCIETY

Enriching Diversity • Shaping Immigration •
Diverse Living Arrangements • Committed Civil Society • Strong Welfare State •
Leisure Time and Travel • Freedom of Religious Worship

INSIGHT
ENRICHING DIVERSITY

With some 81.2 million inhabitants, Germany is the most populous nation in the European Union. The modern, cosmopolitan country has developed into an important immigration country. A good 16.4 million people in Germany have a migratory background. Germany is now among those nations with the most liberal immigration rules. According to a 2014 study by the Organisation for Economic Co-operation and Development (OECD), it is the most popular immigration country after the USA.

Most people in Germany have a high standard of living, on an international comparison, and the corresponding freedom to shape their own lives. The United Nations' Human Development Index (HDI) 2014 ranks Germany sixth of 187 countries. In the Nation Brands Index 2014, an international survey

on the image of 50 countries, Germany tops the scale – also owing to its high values in the areas of quality of life and social justice. Germany considers itself a welfare state, whose primary task is to protect all its citizens.

**New ways of life are
changing the society**

German society is shaped by a pluralism of lifestyles and ethno-cultural diversity. New ways of life and everyday realities are changing daily life in society. Immigrants enrich the country with new perspectives and experiences. There is great social openness and acceptance as regards alternative ways of life and different sexual orientations. Advances are being made in terms of gender equality and traditional gender role assignments are no longer rigid. People with dis- ▶

VIDEO AR APP

Society: the video on the topic
→ **tued.net/en/vid6**

A high standard of living and great individual freedom shape quality of life in Germany

▶ abilities are taking an ever greater role in social life.

Demographic and socioeconomic change

In future, demographic change is set to shape Germany more than virtually any other development. The birth rate has been constantly low since the late 1990s at 1.4 children per woman, and life expectancy is rising. By 2050 the population in Germany is estimated to shrink by around seven million people. At the same time, the growing number of elderly people is presenting social welfare systems with new challenges.

Socioeconomic change in Germany in recent years has led to the emergence of new social risks and stronger social diversification according to economic living conditions. Although in 2014 unemployment was at the same low level as in 1991 (on average 2.7 million), almost one in six in Germany is at risk of poverty, particularly young people and single parents. Moreover, social differences continue to exist between east and west.   ∎

➔ INTERNET

Deutsch plus
Interdisciplinary network and initiative for a pluralist republic
→ deutsch-plus.de

Make it in Germany
Multilingual welcome portal for international skilled workers
→ make-it-in-germany.com

Human Development Reports
Where does Germany stand on a global comparison?
→ hdr.undp.org

Demographic change is presenting the nation with major challenges

PLAYERS & ORGANISATIONS

Federal Office for Migration and Refugees

The Federal Office offers complete information on residence in Germany and makes decisions relating to applications for asylum.

→ bamf.de

German Islam Conference

Since 2006 a long-term dialogue between the German state and Muslims living in Germany has been in place in the form of the German Islam Conference (DIK).

→ deutsche-islam-konferenz.de

Federal Volunteer Service

The service is geared towards women and men who want to get involved in working for the common good – in a social, ecological or cultural context or in sport, integration or civil protection and disaster response.

→ bundesfreiwilligendienst.de

National Action Plan for Integration

Germany seeks to achieve a high level of integration, which is why the topic has been a focal point of the Federal Government's work since 2005. An integration summit takes place annually.

→ bundesregierung.de

Polling institutes

Several established opinion polling institutes regularly survey Germans' opinions and publish projections on election days. Among the best

known are Forschungsgruppe Wahlen, Forsa, Emnid, Infratest Dimap and Institut für Demoskopie Allensbach.

Federal Employment Agency

The national employment agency is responsible for job placement and employment promotion as well as financial compensation.

→ arbeitsagentur.de

Foundations

Germany has one of the highest densities of foundations in Europe. On a national average, there are 26 foundations for every 100,000 inhabitants. The best known is Stiftung Warentest, which tests and compares products on behalf of the government.

→ stiftungen.org

✚ DIGITAL PLUS

More information on all topics in this chapter – link lists with additional comments, articles, documents; plus more detailed information on terms such as demographic change, social security, intergenerational contract, equal rights, and standard of living.

→ tued.net/en/dig6

SHAPING IMMIGRATION

As a destination for migrants, Germany is now among the world leaders. The Organisation for Economic Co-operation and Development (OECD) established that in 2014 Germany was the most popular immigration country in the world after the USA. Among the 34 OECD countries, immigration to Germany has increased the most in recent years. Since Reunification in 1990, 21 million people have come to Germany – with only 16 million moving away in the same period. 2013 saw the highest level of immigration since 1993 at 1.2 million people, and net migration for the year was positive with a plus of 437,000 people.

In total, 7.2 million people with a foreign passport live in Germany. Yet around 16.4 million people have a migratory background. These include immigrants, foreigners born in Germany and people with one immigrant or foreign parent. This group corresponds to a share of just over 20 percent of the total population, around 10.5 million of them immigrated themselves. More than three quarters of immigrants come from another European country. According to the Migration Report, in 2013 most immigrants came from Poland and Romania. The largest ethnic minority in Germany is formed by the almost three million people with Turkish roots (including 1.3 million German nationals).

Many first-generation immigrants came following the labour recruitment agreement with Turkey in 1961 as unqualified workers. Today immigrants of Turkish origin also include students, entrepreneurs and skilled workers. A further large group comes from the former Yugoslavia or its successor states. Today, 56 percent of people with a migratory background have a German passport. In ▶

DIAGRAM

Population according to migration status 2014

Modern immigration society
Germany is the second-most popular destination for immigrants in the world after the United States. In 2014 altogether some 16.4 million people in Germany had a migratory background. There are around four to five million Muslims living in Germany – only roughly half of them consider themselves religious, equating to 2.5 to 3 percent of the population.

7.2 m foreigners

9.2 m people with migratory background and German passport

64.5 m Germans without migratory background

Source: German Federal Statistical Office

Minister of State Aydan Özoğuz is the Federal Government Commissioner for Migration, Refugees and Integration

Net immigration
according to region of origin 2013

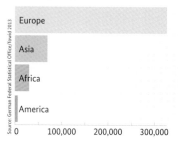

Source: German Federal Statistical Office/fowid 2013

Europe

Asia

Africa

America

0   100,000   200,000   300,000

Religious affiliation in Germany

0.1 %
Jewish communities

0.9 %
Protestant free churches

1.3 %
Orthodox churches

2.2 %
Other

2.6 %
Muslims

34 %
No religious denomination

29.9 %
Roman Catholic Church

28.9 %
Protestant Church

2014, 108,420 foreigners were naturalised. Late emigrants of German extraction from the successor states to the former USSR constitute the largest group of immigrants, numbering around 4.5 million people.

Migrants render an important contribution to social and economic development in Germany. The Federal Government wishes to enable further immigration, also to counter the shortage of skilled labour resulting from demographic change. According to a study by the Bertelsmann Foundation the number of Germans of working age will sink from 45 million to less than 29 million by 2050. Without further immigration, the pressure on social welfare systems will increase. The pension system in particular is based on an intergenerational contract, whereby the working population today finances with its contributions the pensions of the generation that has reached retirement age on a pay-as-you-go principle – with the expectation that the coming generation will later finance their pensions. The growing need for skilled labour is increasingly bringing well qualified migrants to Germany. The proportion of new immigrants with an academic background is above the average proportion of academics in the German population.

The EU Blue Card in particular is a central residence permit facilitating access to the German labour market for skilled academics from non-EU states. Planned legislation is intended to link up immigration rules.

Integration as a key task of migration policy

With the reform of citizenship law in 2014, dual citizenship was introduced and the "option obligation" abolished for the children of foreign parents who were born and grew up in Germany after 1990. Previously they had to decide for one or the other citizenship at the latest upon reaching 23 years of age.

Migrants are becoming ever better integrated in Germany. The immigrant employment

MILESTONES

1955
Strong economic growth leads to a shortage of labour in Germany in the mid-1950s. Recruitment agreements with Italy, Spain, Greece, Turkey, Morocco, Portugal, Tunisia, and Yugoslavia follow.

1964
The millionth migrant worker, called "Gastarbeiter", is welcomed to Germany. Recruitment is halted in 1973 with the oil crisis. Now around four million foreigners are living in Germany.

1990
Immigration increases rapidly in 1990 with the fall of the Iron Curtain and the wars in former Yugoslavia. Moreover, 400,000 people of German origin arrive in Germany from Central and Eastern Europe.

rate has risen by 5 percent since 2007, the strongest rise within the OECD countries. Yet clear deficits are evident particularly in the area of education. The high proportion of young people with foreign roots who can read and write German only poorly is problematic. More than 30 percent of 20 to 29-year-old adults from foreign countries never earn a vocational qualification. Raising their level of participation in the education system is a key goal of the Federal Government.

A further key task of migration and integration policy is protecting refugees. The German Basic Law gives those fleeing political persecution a basic right to asylum. In this way Germany reaffirms its historical and humanitarian responsibility. The number of people seeking asylum has increased significantly of late. Whereas in 2004 around 50,000 people applied for asylum, in 2014 the figure was more than 200,000. Owing to the continual streams of refugees from war-torn and crisis regions in Syria, Iraq and Afghanistan, the expectation is that between 800,000 and

one million applications for political asylum will be filed with the Federal Office for Migration and Refugees (BAMF) by year-end 2015. Germany is facing this challenge and at the same time is committed to finding a Europe-wide solution to the issue of refugees based on solidarity. ∎

🌐 **G L O B A L**

OECD study on the integration of immigrants In recent years Germany has succeeded in integrating immigrants ever better in the labour market. Yet deficits are still evident among children of parents born abroad. These are the findings of a comparative study by the Organisation for Economic Co-operation and Development (OECD) entitled "Indicators of Immigrant Integration 2015".
→ **oecd.org**

1997

Alongside migrant workers, since the mid-1980s ever more asylum seekers have been coming to Germany. From 1997 the Dublin Convention determines responsibilities of the EU states regarding asylum procedures.

2005

The "Microcensus" offers the very first opportunity to survey the migratory background of the population. According to the census, in 2015 every fifth person in Germany has a migratory background.

2014

More than 200,000 people apply for asylum in Germany in 2014. For the first time, almost half a million more people move to Germany than leave it in the same period.

DIVERSE LIVING ARRANGEMENTS

Even in the individualised and highly mobile world of the 21st century, family is accorded a central role. For almost nine out of ten Germans, family continues to be the most important social institution and influential reference group. At the same time ideas about the typical family form are changing. Less than half the people in Germany live in a family unit. Despite the decline of traditional family structures, in 2014 married couples with children under 18 constituted the most common family form at 69 percent. The number of marriages shows a downward trend; in 2013 the figure was 373,600. A little more than one in three marriages ends in divorce. The average length of marriages that ended in divorce in 2013 was 14 years and eight months. Around 44,000 marriages take place between Germans and foreigners.

The number of unmarried couples with children living together is significantly increasing. Between 1996 and 2013 the figure doubled to 8.1 million families today; every tenth couple with a child is unmarried. Families with just one parent are the strongest-growing family form. Today single parents make up a fifth of all parent-child constellations and nine out of ten of the 1.64 million single parents are women. Single parents are often at considerable risk of enduring poverty; 40 percent of them draw state benefits.

Same-sex partnerships are among those forms of living that are gaining in significance. In 2013 there were 78,000 homosexual couples living together in Germany – a third more than ten years previously. Around 35,000 of them live in a registered partnership, which has since 2001 ensured that same-sex couples' relationships are legally recognised.

Whereas on the one hand new forms of cohabitation are emerging, on the other the number of one-person households is on the rise. 41 percent of all private households are single households – 16.5 million people live alone. While this development is a result of demographic change, with the number of elderly people living alone increasing, more young people are also living alone.

**Targeted support for families
with parental leave and family allowance**

Structures are likewise changing within families. Intergenerational relationships between parents and children are often good and as a rule are not characterised by traditional or authoritarian upbringing patterns, but by involvement, affection, encouragement and the promotion of independence. The proportion of working mothers has risen to over 66 percent (2006: 61 percent). More than 70 percent of working women with children work on a part-time basis

Great importance is attached to family – a great many fathers now also take parental leave

however, especially those whose children are not yet at school; the corresponding figure for working fathers is just five percent. In 2014 the employment rate of women in Germany was 73.1 percent, the second-highest figure in the EU and clearly above the EU average (62.3 percent).

The parental leave introduced in 2007 enables couples to more easily reconcile starting a family with professional further development. It is among the numerous benefits designed to assist parents and contribute to a family-friendly society. Parental leave gives both partners the option of suspending their job for up to three years. During this period they receive family allowance for up to 14 months amounting to 67 percent of their last net income (minimum of 300, maximum of 1,800 euros) to secure their livelihood. ▶

New forms of cohabitation, such as in same-sex partnerships, are accepted

▶ **75 percent of** Germans consider family allowance to be a good arrangement; almost all parents take advantage of the benefit. However, four out of five fathers only take the minimum period of two months off. It continues to be primarily mothers who stay at home for a longer period after having children. The Elterngeld Plus family allowance scheme launched in 2015 makes returning to work early on even more worthwhile: Parents who work part-time receive financial support for up to 28 months.

The number of nursery places for under-threes has more than doubled

Since 1 August 2013 children have had a legal right to a nursery place upon reaching the age of one. Today every third child under three (694,500 children in 2015) attends one of the 54,000 day-care facilities or is cared for by one of 44,000 child minders. The number of nursery places for under-threes has more than doubled since 2006.

Parental leave, family allowance, and improved overall conditions for day-care for babies and pre-schoolers continue to create the preconditions for the equal treatment of women as laid down in the Basic Law. Whereas in the education sector young women have not only caught up with, but in part overtaken young men (in 2014 54.4 percent of those attained a university entrance qualification were women, 48.7 percent of new students in 2014/15 were women), there are still differences between the sexes as regards pay and career paths: On average women working full-time only earn around 78 percent of the salary of their male counterparts. They also continue to be underrepresented in managerial roles. According to a study by the German Institute for Economic Research (DIW), of the 877 seats on the executive boards of the top 200 companies, only 47 are occupied by women.

In 2015 the Law on Equal Participation of Women and Men in Leadership Positions entered into force in the private and public sector. Among other things, it stipulates that women must occupy 30 percent of seats on the supervisory councils of companies listed on the stock exchange. In future 3,500 additional firms must set themselves binding targets to increase the proportion of women in managerial positions. The proportion of women in the Bundestag has, in contrast, developed remarkably, currently at 36.5 percent.

Inclusion as an important social responsibility

The Federal Government also aims to create equal opportunities for people with disabilities. It is working towards an inclusive society in which everyone can participate equally: at school, at work, in leisure time. This requires comprehensive accessibility – and the aim is to remove both obstacles in buildings, on streets and paths and social hurdles, such as access to the labour market.

In 2007 Germany was one of the first states to sign the United Nations Convention on the Rights of Persons with Disabilities, with a national action plan structuring its implementation. Among other things, it envisages intensive preparation measures for working life for severely disabled youths. Going beyond the action plan, a federal participation law is envisaged, thus aligning support for people with disabilities even more closely with individual living situations.

The elderly constitute a further group whose needs and potential the Federal Government particularly has in mind. 17 million people in Germany are aged 65 years or older. Their wealth of experience is considered beneficial to society. Their ways of life have likewise diversified and changed; overall elderly people are considerably more active today than in the past. They are frequently also still integrated in the labour market. As meeting places, 450 multigenerational houses promote an intensive dialogue between old and young, bringing together people of different ages. ∎

Ⓡ **I N F O**

Shell Youth Study What makes young people in Germany "tick"? What is important to them, how do they spend their spare time, what is their relationship like to their parents and friends? Since 1953 the oil-and-gas company Shell has regularly commissioned independent research institutes to paint a portrait of young people. The 17th Shell Youth Study is due to be published in October 2015.
→ **shell.de/aboutshell/our-commitment/shell-youth-study.html**

TOPIC
COMMITTED CIVIL SOCIETY

Around 23 million Germans are involved in voluntary work in their spare time, thus assuming responsibility for society. This commitment is often long term – on average volunteers have been active for ten years. Civic commitment is estimated at 4.6 billion hours worked annually. Together with charities, churches, cooperatives, aid organisations, non-profit organisations and private initiatives, the members of the 580,000 associations form the backbone of the "third sector". Civil society refers to the section of society that is not shaped by government or party politics, but gets involved in social and political issues voluntarily and publicly.

Foundations in particular have become increasingly significant. With more than 20,000 incorporated foundations under civil law, the classic legal form of a foundation, Germany has one of the highest numbers of foundations in Europe. Since the turn of the millennium some 12,500 civil-law foundations have been established; more than half of all foundations of this kind in existence today. On a national average, there are 26 foundations for every 100,000 inhabitants. Taken together, all foundations have assets amounting to approximately 70 billion euros. They spend around 17 billion on charitable causes, traditionally social issues (28.8 percent), education, science and culture. The five largest foundations in terms of expenditure are the Volkswagen Foundation, Robert Bosch Stiftung, Bertelsmann Stiftung, Hans Böckler Foundation and WWF Deutschland.

Community foundations are strongly on the rise, foundations in which several citizens and firms act as joint funders to support local or regional projects. The first foundations of this kind were established in 1996 – in mid-2015 there were as many as 275 community foundations recognised by the Association of German Foundations. Civil commitment has slightly increased in recent years, but is shifting more strongly away from the larger associations and towards small, self-organised groups and alternating projects. Currently there are numerous people in Germany involved on a voluntary basis in local initiatives supporting refugees.

Involvement in parties, trade unions, and non-governmental organisations

Socio-political involvement in parties, trade unions and NGOs enables people to help shape things on a strategic and political level. Here volunteering opens a door to intensive democratic participation. The major established organisations however are finding it increasingly difficult to get volunteers on board.

There is particular potential for volunteer work in the 14 to 24-year age bracket. The

Environmental protection is an issue many people actively work for in their spare time

interest in volunteer services shows that young adults are willing to get involved in society. The Federal Volunteer Service has been in place since 2011. It is open to all age groups and complements the model, in existence for over 50 years, of the voluntary social year for young people and young adults. It is also possible to do voluntary work abroad, for example through the International Volunteer Service of the Federal Ministry for Family Affairs, Senior Citizens, Women and Youth, the Weltwärts programme of the Federal Ministry for Economic Cooperation and Development, or the Kulturweit volunteer service by the German UNESCO Commission in cooperation with the German Federal Foreign Office. Considering all services together, in 2014 there were roughly 90,000 to 100,000 volunteers. ∎

TOPIC
STRONG WELFARE STATE

Germany has one of the most comprehensive welfare systems. As in other developed democracies, in Germany too social spending represents the largest individual item of public spending. Around 849 billion euros was committed to public social spending in 2014, equating to a share of 29 percent of gross domestic product (GDP). The tradition of the state welfare system goes back to the age of industrialisation in Germany in the second half of the 19th century and are associated with the then Reich Chancellor Otto von Bismarck. It was under Bismarck that firstly mandatory health insurance for workers was introduced in 1883, and with the social legislation that was expanded in the following years the basis was created for an orientation on the welfare state. The principle of the welfare state is embedded in article 20, paragraph 1 and article 28 of the Basic Law of the Federal Republic of Germany. Politicians and social players must continually renegotiate which form it takes in a dynamic process; particularly demographic change necessitates adjustments.

Social network to protect against existential risks

Today a tightly woven web of state health, pension, accident, nursing care and unemployment insurance protects citizens against the consequences of existential risks and threats. Moreover, the social network encompasses a basic income for pensioners and those permanently unable to work as well as fiscal benefits such as the family allowance system (child benefit, tax advantages). Following a further increase in 2015, families receive 188 euros monthly for the first and second child, 194 euros for the third and 219 euros for additional children.

The pension package that entered into force in 2014 especially improves the situation of elderly people. The reform saw the introduction, among other things, of the full pension from 63 years of age and the so-called mother's pension, intended to serve as an acknowledgement of mothers' work raising children. Women who raised children born before 1992 did not have the

 # NUMBER

30.4 m

is the number of employees subject to mandatory social insurance contributions that the Federal Employment Agency counted in December 2014. This equates to 75 to 80 percent of all employees. The figure does not include those not subject to mandatory social insurance contributions, i.e. civil servants, the self-employed, unpaid family workers and mini-jobbers.
→ statistik.arbeitsagentur.de

With a monthly child allowance, the state specifically promotes families – pre-school childcare provision has been broadened

childcare options available to parents today and as such fewer opportunities in the world of work. The mother's pension acknowledges women's work in raising children. Since July 2014 around 9.5 million women (and a small number of men) have received over 300 euros more in pension payments per child per year. Furthermore, since 1 July 2014 people covered by the pension insurance scheme who have paid in for 45 years have been entitled to retire at 63 without their pension being subject to deductions. Around 280,000 employees took advantage of this option in the first year. The Institute for Employment Research (IAB) expects to receive a good 560,000 applications by the end of 2018.

Health insurance cover is a legal requirement in Germany. Medical care is guaranteed by a broad spectrum of hospitals, practices and rehabilitation clinics. ∎

PANORAMA
LEISURE TIME AND TRAVEL

Popular leisure time activities

Of 100 people polled in Germany in each category, the following number engage in the activities at least once a week:

Watching TV **97**

Listening to the radio **90**

Telephoning from home **89**

Surfing on the Internet **73**

Reading newspapers/magazines **72**

Thinking **71**

Telephoning while out and about **71**

Spending time with their partner **68**

Sleeping in **65**

Talking about important things **64**

Computer **61**

Taking time to pamper oneself **61**

Listening to a CD/MP3 file **54**

Drinking coffee/eating cake **52**

The amount of leisure time Germans have
The amount of time Germans have on a working day to do things they enjoy:

Less than 1 hour	1 to 2 hours	2.5 to 4 hours	4.5 to 6 hours	More than 6 hours
3 %	**18 %**	**38 %**	**17 %**	**23 %**

---

23 million
Germans engage in voluntary activities in their leisure time

43,957
people take part in the Federal Volunteer Service programme

28 million
people in Germany are members of a sports club

94 %
of private households have at least one mobile phone

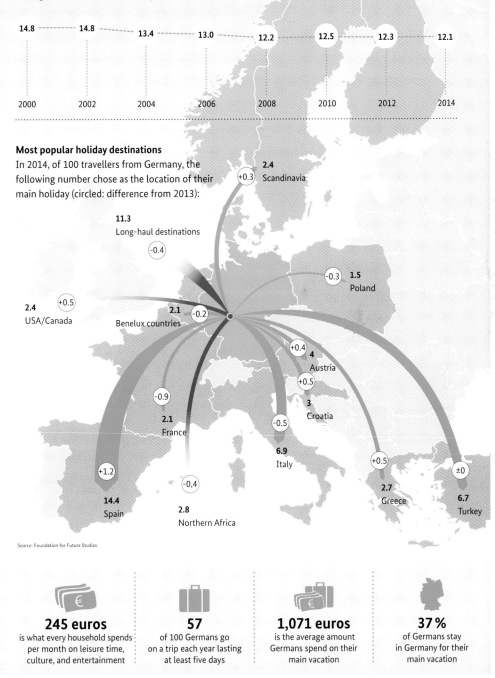

The length of holidays
Average duration of travels in days:

2000	2002	2004	2006	2008	2010	2012	2014
14.8	14.8	13.4	13.0	12.2	12.5	12.3	12.1

Most popular holiday destinations
In 2014, of 100 travellers from Germany, the following number chose as the location of their main holiday (circled: difference from 2013):

2.4 Scandinavia (+0.3)

11.3 Long-haul destinations (−0.4)

1.5 Poland (−0.3)

2.4 USA/Canada (+0.5)

2.1 Benelux countries (−0.2)

4 Austria (+0.4)

3 Croatia (+0.5)

2.1 France (−0.9)

6.9 Italy (−0.5)

14.4 Spain (+1.2)

2.8 Northern Africa (−0,4)

2.7 Greece (+0.5)

6.7 Turkey (±0)

Source: Foundation for Future Studies

245 euros
is what every household spends per month on leisure time, culture, and entertainment

57
of 100 Germans go on a trip each year lasting at least five days

1,071 euros
is the average amount Germans spend on their main vacation

37 %
of Germans stay in Germany for their main vacation

FREEDOM OF RELIGIOUS WORSHIP

The religious landscape in Germany is shaped by increasing plurality and secularisation. 58.8 percent of the German population confesses to one of the two major Christian faiths, organised in the 27 Catholic dioceses and German Bishops' Conference and the Protestant regional churches under the umbrella organisation Evangelical Church in Germany (EKD).

The Catholic Church, with just under 24 million members in 12,000 parishes, is part of the worldwide Roman Catholic Church headed by the Pope. The EKD is a community of 20 independent evangelical regional churches of the Lutheran, Reformed and United confessions. With around 23 million members, they encompass the majority of evangelical Christians. 34 percent of the population does not profess to a particular faith. As a consequence of the ageing membership and high levels of people leaving the Christian churches, the number of believers is falling. In 2014, 218,000 people left the Catholic Church alone. The low number of believers in east Germany is particularly striking.

Islam is gaining in significance for religious life owing to migration. There are an estimated four million Muslims in Germany from 50 different nations, but there is no central survey. Significant Muslim communities have formed in many cities. The German Islam Conference established in 2006 provides an official framework for exchange between Muslims and the German state.

Jewish life in Germany, which was entirely destroyed after the Holocaust, has been revived since the end of the Cold War thanks to migrants from the former USSR. Today around 200,000 Jews live in Germany. Roughly 100,500 of them are organised in 107 Jewish communities, which have a broad religious spectrum and are represented by the Central Council of Jews in Germany, founded in 1950.

Germany has no state church. The basis of the relationship between state and religion

≣ LIST

- Catholic diocese with the most members: **Archdiocese of Cologne with 2,035,000 Catholics**

- Evangelical regional church with the most members: **Hanover with 2,763,633 Protestants**

- Major mosques: **Yavuz Sultan Selim Mosque/Mannheim; Şehitlik Mosque/Berlin, Fatih Mosque/Bremen**

- Largest Jewish community: **Jewish Community of Berlin (10,009)**

In Germany the Basic Law guarantees religious freedom; there are more than 2,000 mosques

is the freedom of religion enshrined in the Basic Law, the separation of church and state in the sense of the state's religious neutrality and the right to self-determination of the religious communities.

The state and religious communities co-operate on a joint basis. The state helps finance nurseries and schools sponsored by religious communities, while churches levy a church tax, collected by the state, to finance social services. Schools must offer religious studies as a regular subject (limited in Berlin and Bremen). Islamic religious instruction is currently being expanded. Around 700,000 Muslim children and young people attend school in Germany. Additional teachers are being trained in order to be able to offer them religious instruction. ∎

CULTURE & THE MEDIA

Vibrant Nation of Culture • Innovative Creative Industry • Intercultural
Dialogue • Cosmopolitan Positions • Rapid Change in the Media •
Exciting World Heritage Sites • Attractive Language

INSIGHT
VIBRANT NATION OF CULTURE

There is no one single German culture. There are many German cultures which simultaneously coexist despite what are often astonishing differences; they are intertwined, repelling and attracting one another. To speak of Germany as a nation of culture in the 21st century is to talk of a mature and continuously developing living organism whose variety is astounding, unsettling, indeed often taxing. This can in part be attributed to the country's federal traditions: After all, Germany was not a unified state until 1871. Not only the Federal Republic of Germany founded in 1949, but also the Germany that was reunified in 1990 has consciously upheld the federal traditions and left the federal states firmly responsible for cultural policy. It was not until 1998 that there was a minister of state in charge of culture and the media attached to the Federal Chancellery. One of the effects of Germany having arisen from many

small and medium-sized states and free cities, there are, amongst other things, around 300 theatres, 130 professional orchestras (which are in some instances paired with radio stations), and 80 musical theatres. Furthermore, 630 art museums with outstanding international collections form an unprecedented gallery scene. Germany is a world leader in terms of sheer variety in cultural facilities. The population generally welcomes the fact that theatres, orchestras and museums are predominantly public institutions run by the federal states. Against the backdrop of public budget constraints, sociodemographic change and shifts in the media landscape (such as digitisation) the cultural system is currently in a phase of upheaval and reorientation.

Germany's reputation as a major cultural nation rests on the great names of the past, ▶

VIDEO ◧ AR APP

Culture & The Media: the video on the
topic → **tued.net/en/vid7**

The future centre for dialogue between the world's cultures: the Humboldt Forum is under construction in Berlin

▶ such as Bach, Beethoven and Brahms in music, Goethe, Schiller and Thomas Mann in literature. Moreover, there are exceptional examples of German Modernists in all art genres.

It bears noting that the country has gone through a process which began earlier in other European nations. Germany has embraced outside influences on the basis of its own traditions and developed a new narrative. Young artists from migratory backgrounds have found expressive means, both poetic and musical, to respond to the encounter and fusion of different cultural backgrounds.

The regional artistic and cultural centres have morphed into vibrant centres of new German culture in the increasingly blurred grey area between low-brow and high-brow culture. Together they create a force field, a reflection of Germany in concentrated form. There is also the Humboldt Forum project, which will open in 2019 as a cultural lighthouse in the rebuilt palace in central Berlin. Characterised by cosmopolitanism, it should facilitate an international exchange of knowledge and intercultural dialogue. ▪

→ INTERNET

Kulturportal Deutschland
Website on selected events and cultural policy issues
→ kulturportal-deutschland.de

Litrix
Multilingual information portal to present German literature worldwide
→ litrix.de

Filmportal
Platform on movies in German
→ filmportal.de

There are many venues in Germany for the performing arts

PLAYERS & ORGANISATIONS

German Federal Government Commissioner for Culture and the Media

The German Federal Government Commissioner for Culture and the Media, Monika Grütters, is, as Minister of State, a member of the Federal Chancellery. Her tasks include promoting cultural institutions and projects that are of national significance.

→ **bundesregierung.de**

Goethe-Institut

Goethe-Institut e.V. is Germany's globally active cultural institute. Its brief is to promote a knowledge of the German language abroad, nurture international cultural cooperation and convey an exhaustive current image of Germany.

→ **goethe.de**

Institute for Foreign Cultural Relations

The Institute for Foreign Cultural Relations (ifa) dedicates itself world-wide to interaction on art, civil society dialogue, and providing information on foreign cultural policy.

→ **ifa.de**

Kulturstiftung des Bundes

The Kulturstiftung des Bundes promotes art and culture that falls within the ambit of the Federal Government. One focal point is supporting innovative programmes and projects in the international context.

→ **kulturstiftung-des-bundes.de**

Haus der Kulturen der Welt

Haus der Kulturen der Welt in Berlin is a centre of international cultural exchange and a forum for contemporary debates.

→ **hkw.de**

Deutscher Kulturrat

Deutscher Kulturrat e.V. is the acknowledged umbrella association of German cultural associations, with 246 federal cultural associations and organisations forming its membership.

→ **kulturrat.de**

Central Agency for German Schools Abroad

The Central Agency for German Schools Abroad (ZfA) promotes and advises 1,200 schools abroad, including 140 German schools abroad.

→ **auslandsschulwesen.de**

✚ DIGITAL PLUS

For details on all the topics in this chapter – commented lists of links, articles, documents, speeches; and for further information on keywords such as the federal state's responsibility for culture, Kulturstiftung des Bundes, Deutscher Filmpreis, documenta.

→ **tued.net/en/dig7**

TOPIC
INNOVATIVE CREATIVE INDUSTRY

Culture and the creative industry are among the economy's most innovative sectors. In Germany, their contribution to total economic output (gross value added) is steadily increasing and today is already on a par with major sectors of industry, such as mechanical engineering. Sales by the creative industries, which now embrace some 249,000 companies and in which 1.5 million people work, totalled around 145 billion euros in 2013.

The common core of work in culture and the creative industries is the creative act underlying artistic, literary, cultural, musical, architectural and creative content, works, products, productions, and services. Structurally speaking, the sector is defined by self-employed freelancers, and small or micro-enterprises (97 percent). They are primarily private-sector based – meaning not first and foremost in the public sector (museums, theatre, orchestras) or part of civil society (arts, associations, foundations). Through the consistent promotion of start-ups, in many cities a raft of service providers has arisen in the fields of design, software and games in particular. Specifically, the software and games industry relies on interfacing different segments, such as film, video, music, text and animation, to tap the sector's potential and in 2013 this spawned total sales of 31 billion euros. The Berlin-Brandenburg region leads the way, with a good 200 companies. No other area has such a concentrated gaming infrastructure, including the relevant colleges. That said, Frankfurt/Main, Hamburg, Leipzig, Cologne and Munich all have clear creative industry clusters. A closely interlocking range of consultancies, networks and grants provides an ideal basis for this, along with high-performance IT infrastructures. ■

📈 DIAGRAM

Steady growth: companies in the cultural and creative sectors

Sector with great potential
The cultural and creative industries bring traditional segments of business together with new technologies and modern forms of ICT. In Germany it includes 12 sub-segments: the music business, bookselling, the art market, the film industry, radio, the fine arts, architecture, design, the press, advertising, software/games, others.

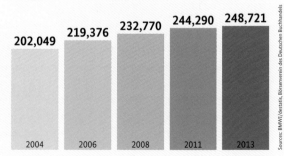

202,049 — 2004
219,376 — 2006
232,770 — 2008
244,290 — 2011
248,721 — 2013

Sources: BMWi/destatis, Börsenverein des Deutschen Buchhandels

Berlin is considered the start-up capital, among young entrepreneurs, too

Highly varied book market: many new publications

6.3 %
Travel

9.0 %
Schools & learning

9.3 %
Non-fiction

11.3 %
Science

14.5 %
Self-help books

81,919
New publications

33.8 %
Literature

15.8 %
Books for children
and young people

Well placed in the middle of the table: gross value added by sector in million €

Sector	Value
Chemicals industry	**40.3**
Energy utilities	**54.9**
Culture and the creative sector	**63.6**
Financial service providers	**67.8**
Mechanical engineering	**87.9**
Automobile industry	**110.4**

TOPIC
INTERCULTURAL DIALOGUE

Alongside classical diplomacy and foreign economic policy, cultural relations and education policy forms the third pillar of German foreign policy. Its key objectives include laying strong foundations for relations to other countries and fostering dialogue among people and peoples by means of exchanges and cooperation in the fields of culture, education and scholarship. The foreign cultural policy thus paves the way for mutual understanding, an important bedrock for policies committed to the peaceful settlement of differences. Other tasks include promoting the German language around the world, showcasing Germany as a country with a successful and diverse cultural scene, and communicating a contemporary image of Germany abroad.

≡ LIST

• Largest art museum:
Hamburger Kunsthalle

• Largest orchestra:
Gewandhausorchester Leipzig

• Largest movie theatre:
Cinemaxx in Essen

• Largest theatre stage:
Friedrichstadtpalast (Berlin)

• Largest festival hall:
Baden-Baden

Actual initiatives include promoting a variety of cultural programmes, such as exhibitions, guest performances by German theatres, supporting literature and films, and baking projects in dialogue with the Islamic world or kulturweit, a scheme that enables young people from Germany to spend a year doing voluntary service abroad.

The programmes and projects rest on a comprehensive understanding of culture

The Federal Foreign Office only implements the smallest part of its cultural relations policy itself. It primarily entrusts these tasks to intermediary organisations active as entities under private law and each with its own special focus. They include the Goethe-Institut, Institute for Foreign Cultural Relations (ifa), the German Academic Exchange Service (DAAD), the German Commission for UNESCO, and the Alexander von Humboldt Foundation (on foreign education policy, please turn to the chapter on Education and Knowledge).

The work of the cultural intermediaries is defined in agreements on goals, but they are largely free to structure the programmes and projects themselves. The Goethe-Institut has a total of 159 institutes in 98 different countries. It promotes a knowledge of the German language abroad and nurtures international cultural cooperation. The ifa dedicates itself

Old manuscripts from Timbuktu (Mali) are being preserved and researched thanks to Federal Foreign Office funding

mainly to cultural dialogue – in the form of exhibitions and conferences. The current trends in cultural dialogue: digital cultural and intermediary services and the new opportunities for interactive participation. In all the projects, since the 1970s foreign cultural policy has emphasised a holistic, non-elitist concept of culture that does not limit "culture" to "art".

That said, the focus is not just on German culture. The preservation of cultural heritage programmes supports upholding important historical cultural assets worldwide. For example, from 1981 to 2015 the Federal Foreign Office has helped fund more than 2,700 projects in 144 countries, including the preservation of the Timbuktu manuscripts in Mali, the creation of a digital registry of cultural assets for Syria, the digitisation of traditional music in Cameroon and reconstructing the Great Hall of Karakorum in Mongolia. ∎

TOPIC
COSMOPOLITAN POSITIONS

In German society, which is steeped in pluralism, there can just as little be one predominant cultural trend as there can be one metropolis that towers over all the others. Buttressed by the country's federal structure, Germany is typified by the simultaneity of many exceptionally different things from different periods, indeed even countervailing or competing currents – in theatre, film, music, the visual arts, and literature.

There is a clear trend in theatre: The number of premiere performances by contemporary playwrights has soared. They run the entire gamut of current forms of the performing arts, in which traditional spoken theatre mingles with pantomime, dance, video, play acting, and music, giving rise to dense performance-like, post-drama stage work. The sheer variety presented each year at the May Berlin Theatertreffen can be read as the polyphonic response to the issues raised by a complex reality.

Alongside the cultural mainstream driven by the centre-ground in society new things are arising, increasingly from marginalised sections of society, and these ideas are penetrating and enriching the established world of theatre. "Postmigrant" is the buzzword describing the phenomenon, reflecting that Germany is an immigration society as is visible in many cities, especially in Berlin. Millions of Germans with a migrant background are the second or third generation of their family living here, they tell tales of themselves and the lives of their parents and grandparents, unlike the stories told by citizens who have lived in Germany for centuries. Whether they were born in Germany or not, as a rule they are not influenced by some hands-on experience of immigration, but by the experience of cultural hybridity. This life in various cultural contexts engenders new forms of artistic enquiry into society and draws up new front lines for negotiating rights, a sense of belonging, or participation. New narratives arise that encourage society to view itself in a new light and define how German culture is perceived abroad.

A beacon of such art that celebrates trans-culturalism is Shermin Langhoff's Post-Migrant

> ⊛ **INFO**
>
> **Adelbert von Chamisso Prize**
> The Adelbert von Chamisso Prize is a literary award bestowed since 1985 by the Robert Bosch Stiftung. It is given to a published work whose author's mother tongue is not German. In 2015, the prize went to Sherko Fatah, a German writer with Iraqi roots (for his oeuvre), to Olga Grjasnova, who was born in Baku/Azerbaijan (for her: Die juristische Unschärfe einer Ehe) and to Martin Kordic (for Wie ich mir das Glück vorstelle), whose father comes from Croatia.
> → bosch-stiftung.de

Yael Ronen's production of Common Ground at the Maxim Gorki Theatre made a real splash

Theatre in Berlin's Maxim Gorki Theatre, the city's smallest state theatre but one with a long-standing tradition. Langhoff's shows reach out well beyond traditional theatre-goers and have successfully attracted a new and primarily young clientele; they reflect an opaque process that is constantly shifting and becoming more differentiated. In 2015, the Gorki Theatre was invited to present the play Common Ground, which addresses the war in the Balkans, produced by Israeli director Yael Ronen, at the Berlin Theatertreffen. Theatre is thus now doing what has long since taken place in the worlds of Pop music and literature. Here, too, the biographies of the artists reflect society's diversity, presenting exciting fusions of widely differing styles to offer new perspectives. In Pop, a whole array of international styles of music, ranging from Balkan beats, Afro-American sounds and ▶

▸ Turkish Saz Rock to American Hip Hop and even Techno, blends with other strands or electronic elements that are considered "typically German". As in other countries, Rap is a point of identification for young people from migrant families, with languages often blurring in the process.

Post-migrant themes play a key role in contemporary literature

There are countless important authors with migrant backgrounds such as Navid Kermani, who in 2015 won one of Germany's most illustrious cultural prizes, the Peace Prize of the German Book Trade, and is known both for his fiction and for his books on religious tolerance, or Katja Petrowskaya, Sherko Fatah, Nino Haratischwili, Saša Stanišić, Feridun Zaimoglu or Alina Bronsky, to mention but a few. Indeed, it is fair to say that for many

years now they have been among the most successful authors writing in German. Their books, which reflect among other things on their experiences with their Iranian, Russian and Turkish backgrounds, are eagerly read and their works transport the specific themes and experiences of migration into the heart of society, where they are regularly discussed.

The same is true of films by directors Fatih Akin or Bora Dagtekin, who playfully have the different milieus so typical of Germany today, and the clichéd notions the various groups have of one another collide. The image of Germany that this creates, reflected at countless different levels, is at times chaotic and contradictory, but always colourful. Society needs to learn to tolerate these ambivalences and tensions; culture shows this and provides an ideal venue for a peaceful debate on these conflicts. Post-migrant Germany is

German-Iranian writer Navid Kermani won the 2015 Peace Prize of the German Book Trade

❶ Golden Bear
The Berlin International Film Festival: one of the world's key film festivals next to Venice and Cannes. A Golden Bear and several Silver Bears are awarded.

❷ Preis der Leipziger Buchmesse
Preis der Leipziger Buchmesse is a book prize awarded to a new publication in German.

❸ Deutscher Filmpreis
Featuring prize money totalling almost 3 million euros, Deutscher Filmpreis is the best endowed German cultural prize.

❹ German Book Prize
A jury chooses the best novel written in German that year.

❺ Georg Büchner Preis
The Georg Büchner Preis is the pre-eminent literature prize for Germany, Austria and Switzerland.

not necessarily cosy, but it is certainly exciting and dynamic.

The visual arts in Germany are likewise cosmopolitan and international. As the statistics of the new intake at German art academies and colleges shows: In 2013, the number of new students coming from abroad for the first time exceeded that of Germans. Today Berlin, with about 500 galleries and its many spaces for presenting artistic positions, is considered the metropolis for young, contemporary art that features strongly in the Berlin Art Week, when all over the city venues present the latest artistic ideas. Indeed, Germany's capital is today undoubtedly one of the world's largest hubs where contemporary art is produced. This is demonstrated every two years at the Venice Biennale, and not just in the German Pavilion there: A large number of the international artists exhibited in the city on the lagoon state that they live in Berlin. ∎

TOPIC
RAPID CHANGE IN THE MEDIA

Freedom of the press and the media is guaranteed at a very high level in Germany, and is protected by the constitution. Article 5 of the Basic Law states: "Every person shall have the right freely to express and disseminate his opinions in speech, writing and pictures, and to inform himself without hindrance from generally accessible sources. ... There shall be no censorship." The Press Freedom Index compiled by the NGO Reporter ohne Grenzen ranks Germany 12th of 180 countries in 2015. There is a diversity of opinions and a pluralism of information. The press is not controlled by governments or parties, as private-sector media corporations are responsible for it. The public broadcasters based on the British model (ARD, ZDF, Deutschlandfunk) as corporate bodies paid for from licensing fees and as public-sector entities are the second pillar of the media world, which rests on the dual principle of private and public-sector entities that has essentially remained unchanged since the foundation of the Federal Republic of Germany in 1949. As of 2015, the monthly license fee has been 17.50 euros. Since the 1980s, there has been a whole raft of private radio and TV broadcasters in the market, and in 2014 each household was able to receive on average 78 TV channels; in total, if one includes the numerous pay-TV offerings, there are over 400 channels. The most important TV news programmes are Tagesschau and Tagesthemen, both on ARD, heute and heute journal on ZDF, and RTL aktuell. In Berlin alone, which is among the 10 top media cities worldwide, there are 900 accredited parliamentary correspondents and 400 foreign correspondents from 60 different countries on the ground.

The many different media voices include 329 daily newspapers, mainly distributed ▶

▯ MILESTONES

1945
After the end of Nazi rule, in Germany initially newspapers may only appear under Allied licence. In the US zone of occupation the first licence is awarded on 1 August 1945 to the Frankfurter Rundschau.

1950
The six West German broadcasting houses agree in Bremen to join forces to form the "Arbeitsgemeinschaft der öffentlichrechtlichen Rundfunkanstalten der Bundesrepublik Deutschland," or ARD broadcaster.

1984
In Ludwigshafen the Programmgesellschaft für Kabel- und Satellitenrundfunk, or PKS for short, starts broadcasting. This marks the birth of private TV channels in Germany.

Social media are fundamentally changing the structure of the media, communications patterns and the public sphere

1995

The first German newspaper, namely the leftist/liberal taz, goes online only six years after the foundation of the World Wide Web. After its go-live, the membership of the digitaz community surges.

1997

About 4.1 million German citizens over the age of 14 use the new online access channels at least occasionally. In 2014, the figure rises to around 55.6 million, or 79.1 percent of the over-14s in Germany.

2014

Some 28 million people in Germany use Facebook. An Allensbach study mentions 1 million Germans who twitter frequently. The leading social media site is WhatsApp, with a good 35 million users.

Germany's largest newsroom: the central editorial desk at Deutsche Presse-Agentur (dpa) in Berlin

▶ regionally, 20 weeklies, and 1,590 mass-mar-ket magazines (2014). After China, India, Japan and the USA, Germany is the fifth-largest newspaper market worldwide. Per publication day, 17.54 million dailies and five million weekly or Sunday papers are sold (2014). The leading nationwide newspapers are Süddeutsche Zeitung, Frankfurter Allgemeine Zeitung, Die Welt, Die Zeit, taz and Handelsblatt, and all stand out for investigative research, analysis, background, and comprehensive commentary. News magazine Spiegel/Spiegel Online and the yellow-press publication Bild are considered the most-quoted media.

At the same time, the sector is undergoing a profound structural change. For the last 15

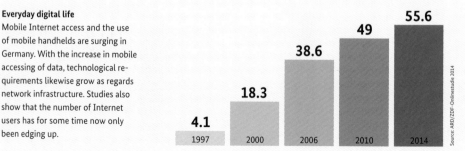

◢ DIAGRAM

Everyday digital life
Mobile Internet access and the use of mobile handhelds are surging in Germany. With the increase in mobile accessing of data, technological requirements likewise grow as regards network infrastructure. Studies also show that the number of Internet users has for some time now only been edging up.

Rapid development: more than 55 million people online in Germany

1997	2000	2006	2010	2014
4.1	18.3	38.6	49	55.6

Source: ARD/ZDF-Onlinestudie 2014

years, newspapers have been regularly losing on average 1.5-2 percent of their paid printed editions. They are increasingly rarely reaching younger readers and with circulation figures and advertising revenues dwindling are in difficult waters. Over 100 newspapers have responded to the free-for-view Internet by introducing pay-on-demand systems.

Digitisation of the media world, the Internet, the rampant growth in mobile handhelds, and the triumphs of the social media have significantly changed how the media are used. Today, 55.6 million Germans over the age of 14 (79 percent) are online. In 2014, every Internet user was online on 5.9 days of the week and spent about 166 minutes a day on the Internet; every second person surfed from a mobile handheld. Moreover, over half of all Internet users are members of a private community. The digital revolution has generated a new concept of the public sphere; the social media and the Bloggosphere mirror an open society of dialogue in which everyone can participate in the opinion-forming discourse.

🌐 **GLOBAL**

Deutsche Welle Deutsche Welle (DW) is Germany's state-run foreign radio service and a member of ARD, the public radio and TV broadcasting association. DW broadcasts in 30 different languages, provides TV programming (DW-TV), radio and Internet services as well as supporting international media development through the DW Akademie. In 2015, the foreign broadcasting service commenced 24/7 programming in English.
→ **dw.de**

Whether the interactive Internet nodes where people gather also form the foundations for a viable future digital journalism remains to be seen. In Germany, for example, the progress of the online magazine Krautreporter, launched by crowdfunding in 2014, is being followed with bated breath. ∎

Multiple access: how Germans use the Internet

95% Computer, PC, laptop

18% TV

28% Tablet

62% Smartphone/ mobile phone

Source: ARD/ZDF-Onlinestudie 2014

Daily media usage

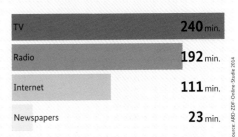

TV	**240** min.
Radio	**192** min.
Internet	**111** min.
Newspapers	**23** min.

Source: ARD-ZDF-Online-Studie 2014

🗔 PANORAMA
EXCITING WORLD HERITAGE SITES

⓱ Cologne Cathedral
This masterpiece of Gothic architecture was built down through many generations – from 1248 to 1880.

㉑ Wartburg
Reformer Martin Luther translated the New Testament into German inside the protection of its walls.

㉕ Zollverein Coal Mine Industrial Complex
This complex in Essen where operations were discontinued in 1986 stands for the development of heavy industry in Europe.

⓲ Bauhaus
The Bauhaus sites in Dessau and Weimar stand for the famous early 20th-century design college.

157 m
Height of Cologne Cathedral

1 km²
Area of the Zollverein Coal Mine Industrial Complex

44 km²
Area covered by ancient beech forests

3,000,000
Visitors to Museum Island

● Cultural heritage sites
● Natural heritage sites

Sleswig-Holstein
33
8
26
Mecklenburg-West Pomerania
34
26
Bremen 33
40
34
Hamburg
28
Lower Saxony
Saxony-Anhalt
22
34
Berlin
9
32
6
23
Brandenburg
35
11
39
14
18
19
25
North Rhine-Westphalia
38
34
19
29
17
34
21
18
20
Saxony
1
5
Hessen
Thuringia
27
16
Rhineland-Palatinate
7
10
3
12
37
Saarland
15
2
30
Bavaria
13
31
Baden-Wurttemberg
36
24
4

1 Aachen Cathedral
2 Speyer Cathedral
3 Würzburg Residence with the Court Gardens and Residence Square
4 Pilgrimage Church of Wies
5 Castles of Augustusburg and Falkenlust at Brühl
6 St Mary's Cathedral and St Michael's Church at Hildesheim
7 Roman Monuments, Cathedral of St Peter and Church of Our Lady in Trier
8 Hanseatic City of Lübeck
9 Palaces and Parks of Potsdam and Berlin
10 Abbey and Altenmünster of Lorsch
11 Mines of Rammelsberg, Historic Town of Goslar and Upper Harz Water Management System
12 Town of Bamberg
13 Maulbronn Monastery Complex
14 Collegiate Church, Castle and Old Town of Quedlinburg
15 Völklingen Ironworks
16 Messel Pit Fossil Site
17 Cologne Cathedral
18 Bauhaus and its sites in Weimar and Dessau
19 Luther Memorials in Eisleben and Wittenberg
20 Classical Weimar
21 Wartburg Castle
22 Museumsinsel (Museum Island), Berlin
23 Garden Kingdom of Dessau-Wörlitz
24 Monastic Island of Reichenau
25 Zollverein Coal Mine Industrial Complex in Essen
26 Historic Centres of Stralsund and Wismar
27 Upper Middle Rhine Valley
28 Town Hall and Roland on the Marketplace of Bremen
29 Muskauer Park / Park Mużakowski
30 Frontiers of the Roman Empire
31 Old town of Regensburg with Stadtamhof
32 Berlin Modernism Housing Estates
33 Wadden Sea
34 Ancient Beech Forests of Germany
35 Fagus Factory in Alfeld
36 Prehistoric Pile dwellings around the Alps
37 Margravial Opera House Bayreuth
38 Bergpark Wilhelmshöhe
39 Carolingian Westwork and Civitas Corvey
40 Speicherstadt and Kontorhaus District with Chilehaus

30 Frontiers of the Roman Empire
The Saalburg castle within the Roman frontier wall in Hessen has been reconstructed.

34 Ancient Beech Forests
Five beech forests in Germany are included on the UNESCO World Heritage List.

2,000
Half-timbered buildings in Quedlinburg

550 km
Length of the Roman frontier wall

10,000
Different animal and plant species in the Wadden Sea

1,031
UNESCO World Heritage sites worldwide

TOPIC
ATTRACTIVE LANGUAGE

German is one of the 15 or so Germanic languages, a branch of the Indo-European language family. About 130 million people in Germany, Austria, Switzerland, Luxembourg, Belgium, Liechtenstein and South Tyrol (Italy) speak German natively or as a regularly used second language. It is therefore the most widely spoken native language in the EU and one of the ten most widely spoken languages. The 2015 survey on 'German as a foreign language worldwide' refers to a total of 15.4 million people currently learning German as a second language. The number of people globally who actually speak German as a foreign language can only be roughly estimated at about 100 million.

One reason why German's importance is disproportionally high relative to the number of people speaking it stems from the country's economic strength, which makes the language very desirable. This desirability is helping drive an active policy of spreading the German language: by supporting language teaching facilities in Germany and abroad; providing scholarships or making academic offers to mobile international students. It is also clear from the significantly increasing interest in German, especially in the rising powers of China, India and Brazil as well as in other fast-growing areas of the Asian continent, where in places demand has quadrupled since 2010.

Important institutions for German learning include the 140 German schools outside Germany and the almost 2,000 schools that lay emphasis on German lessons, which are included in the Federal Foreign Office's initiative, Schools: Partners for the Future (PASCH). In 2014, around 228,000 people took language courses at the Goethe-Institut, which offers German as a foreign language and language tests in more than 90 countries. Around 1.3 million people learn German at universities in 108 countries.

By contrast, the relevance of German as a language of international scholarship is essentially declining. The global share of articles in German in scientific publications forms only one Per cent in bibliographic databases. German enjoys greater importance as a language of scholarship in the

 # NUMBER

16

major dialect associations exist in Germany, including, for example, Bavarian, Alemannic, Westphalian, Brandenburg and Northern Low German. The regional differences in spoken language are fairly large; in general the importance of dialects is dwindling.

The German language is the most frequently spoken mother tongue in the European Union

humanities and social sciences. Non-German-speaking scholars only very rarely publish in German, whereas German-speaking scholars by contrast publish extensively in English, particularly in the sciences. On the Internet, however, the German language plays an important role. With regard to the most used languages there, based on Websites German was in third place in 2015, a long way behind English, but only just behind Russian.

Globalisation is exerting pressure on all international languages, and this is serving to appreciably further strengthen the position of English as the world language. But German will nonetheless remain an important international language. ∎

WAY OF LIFE

Land of Diversity • Urban Quality of Life • Sustainable Tourism •
Sporting Challenges • Leisurely Enjoyment

INSIGHT
LAND OF DIVERSITY

A love of nature and cities alike, healthy food and gourmet restaurants, a strong sense of tradition and a cosmopolitan mindset – measuring 357,000 square kilometres, Germany is the fourth largest country in the European Union (EU) after France, Spain and Sweden. From the North and Baltic Seas to the Alps in the south, Germany is geographically sub-divided into the North German Lowlands, the Mittelgebirge ridge, the Central Uplands in southwest Germany, the South German Alpine foothills and the Bavarian Alps. From north to south the greatest distance is 876 kilometres, from east to west 640 kilometres.

Germany is one of the countries with the highest standards of living in the world. The 2014 United Nations' Human Development Index (HDI) puts Germany sixth out of a total of 187 countries. With 81.2 million inhabitants, Germany is the most populous country in the EU and one of the most densely populated; around 77 percent of its inhabitants live in densely and highly populated areas. Around 30 percent of the population resides in big cities with more than 100,000 inhabitants, of which there are 76 in Germany; Munich has 4,460 people per square kilometre, Berlin 3,780. Experts believe the ongoing trend of growth and innovation is reflected in the renaissance of cities, and forecast that by 2030 the number of inhabitants in major cities will have surged – with considerable consequences for the housing market, inner-city mobility, and infrastructure. In particular, the 18-to-24-year-old age bracket is showing a pronounced willingness to move to cities. This urbanisation makes Germany part of a global trend. The cities are also great tourist attractions – Berlin especially is developing ▶

VIDEO ▶ AR APP

Way of life: the video on the topic
→ **tued.net/en/vid8**

Sylt, the fourth-largest German island, offers kilometres of sandy beaches along the North Sea coast

▶ into a real magnet and is currently setting one visitor record after another. In the European rankings for the absolute number of overnight stays, Berlin, with its 3.4 million inhabitants, places third behind London and Paris.

At the same time, however, this longing for urban life contrasts with a strong call for things regional – in particular when it comes to what Germans eat. The organic food industry is firmly established in German agriculture, generating sales of organic products worth 7.6 billion euros annually. Indeed, 23,500 organic farms, 8 percent of agricultural enterprises, cultivate 6.3 percent of agricultural land. The organic products are supported by certifications (around 70,400 products boast the German state organic seal), extensive consumer protection laws, and comprehensive marking obligations. In 2014, 7.75 million people in Germany, Austria and Switzerland referred to themselves as vegetarians; 900,000 said they live a vegan lifestyle. Gourmets, however, do not miss out. This is thanks to the 282 restaurants in Germany with one or more stars in the 2015 Guide Michelin – the number of them has risen by 25 percent since 2010. ■

➡ **INTERNET**

Destatis
Data, facts and official statistical studies, compiled by the German Federal Statistical Office in Wiesbaden
→ destatis.de

OECD
Comparison of the material living conditions and the quality of life in 34 countries based on the Better Life Index of the Organisation for Economic Co-operation and Development (OECD)
→ oecdbetterlifeindex.org

Frankfurt am Main, home to the European Central Bank (ECB), is the only major German city to boast a skyline

PLAYERS & ORGANISATIONS

German National Tourist Board

For over 60 years the German National Tourist Board (DZT) has been working internationally on behalf of the Federal Government to promote Germany as a travel destination. In 2016, the DZT is focussing on the theme year "The Fascination of a Nature Holiday in Germany – Nature and National Parks".

→ **germany.travel**

German Olympic Sports Confederation

The German Olympic Sports Confederation (DOSB) is the umbrella organisation of German sport. It has more than 28 million members in around 91,000 sports clubs.

→ **dosb.de**

German Football Association

With 6.85 million members, the German Football Association (DFB) is the world's largest national sports federation – and the only football association where both the men's and the women's team have won the World Cup.

→ **dfb.de**

International Sports Promotion

International Sports Promotion has been part of the Federal Republic of Germany's cultural relations and education activities abroad since 1961. Since then it has supported 1,400 short and long-term projects in over 100 developing countries. It primarily promotes women's, disabled, and youth sports, to help integration.

→ **sport.diplo.de**

German Wine Institute

The German Wine Institute (DWI) is the German wine industry's communications and marketing arm. Its main task is to promote the quality and sales of German wine.

→ **deutscheweine.de**

Gut leben in Deutschland

In 2015, the Federal government launched a dialogue with the people in Germany about their view of the quality of life in the country. In events up and down the country and online it discusses matters directly with citizens, so as in future to be able to gear its action more specifically to what is important to the people in Germany.

→ **gut-leben-in-deutschland.de**

✚ DIGITAL PLUS

More information about all the topics in the chapter – annotated link lists, articles, documents; plus more detailed information about terms such as German cuisine, wines from Germany, Bauhaus architecture, wellness holidays in Germany.

→ **tued.net/en/dig8**

TOPIC
URBAN QUALITY OF LIFE

Good jobs, a clean environment, low crime rates, lots of leisure-time and cultural attractions, good transport links: German cities frequently boast precisely these features. In a 2015 study aimed at evaluating the quality of life in 230 large cities conducted by the Mercer consulting firm, seven German cities place in the Top 30. With Munich (4th place), Düsseldorf (6) and Frankfurt am Main (7), three actually make the Top Ten. Berlin (14), Hamburg (16) and Stuttgart (21) are also well up the list. In Germany there are 76 large cities (more than 100,000 inhabitants) and 600 medium-sized cities with between 20,000 and 99,999 inhabitants; 74 percent of people now live in cities.

The demand for urban living space has led to a sharp rise in rents in the case of first-time lets, and in the price of real estate. With regard to European home ownership rates, Germany comes second from last.

Only 43 percent of households live in their own four walls. The majority opt for rented accommodation, which has traditionally always been preferred. Almost 20 percent of people views the cost of living as a "heavy financial burden". On average, such costs absorb 35 percent of monthly incomes. For this reason the Federal Government has paved the way for rent caps aimed at preserving social diversity in regions where the housing market is under pressure. In the event of a change in tenant, new rents are capped at a max. 10 percent higher than for a comparable flat – but there are exceptions. In Berlin 22 areas were given "environment protection". All redevelopment measures, meaning all demolition work, as well as all alterations and changes in use are checked and require approval, in order to prevent refurbishment becoming synonymous with gentrification. This way, so the hope, urban diversity will be preserved. ∎

〰 DIAGRAM

How Germans live
More than half of the people in Germany live in rented accommodation, not in their own four walls. 64.5 percent of all residential buildings are single-family dwellings, only 5.9 percent are larger structures with seven or more flats. 35 percent of flats and houses are 100 square metres in size or bigger, only 5.5 percent of flats are smaller than 40 square metres.

Consumer spending by private households in Germany

22% Other items

4% Clothing, shoes

11% Leisure time, entertainment, culture

35% Accommodation, energy, accommodation maintenance

14% Transportation

14% Food, drink, tobacco

Source: Federal Statistical Office 2014

Urban quality of life is in vogue, which is why rents are rising in cities

Share of the population living in cities

Sources: World Bank, Federal and State Stat. Offices 2013

Germany	**74.2** %
Great Britain	**79.9** %
Canada	**80.9** %
USA	**82.9** %
Australia	**89.5** %

Flats in Germany by number of rooms

25.8 %
4 rooms

39.3 %
5 and more
rooms

3.3 %
1 room

22.2 %
3 rooms

9.4 %
2 rooms

TOPIC
SUSTAINABLE TOURISM

Germans like to travel. In their own country as well, indeed especially there. After all, for years now the Alps, the coasts, the North German lakes, nature reserves, and river valleys have headed the list of destinations. Germans have long since shared a passion for the diversity of the countryside, and for sightseeing, sport and relaxation options with a continually growing flow of visitors and tourists from abroad. Germany has for years been gaining popularity as a tourist destination.

In 2014, the number of overnights rose to 424 million; guests from abroad accounted for 75.6 million (17.8 percent), which was a record. The positive trend in tourism to Germany began immediately after German Reunification back in 1990 and has since led to a steady rise in the number of overnight stays by foreign guests – by around 88 percent or 33.7 million. A good 75 percent of all foreign guests come from Europe, primarily from the Netherlands, Switzerland, Great Britain, and Italy.

At the same time the number of visitors from Asian countries, particularly China and India, as well as from the Arab Gulf States is rising twice as fast, and they now account for over 11 percent of the total. Almost 10 percent of foreign guests come from North and South America. In Europe, since 2010 Germany has been second in the league of most popular destinations among Europeans – after Spain and ahead of France. Seasonal distribution reveals peak figures from June to October during the high season, and regional distribution very high numbers for Bavaria, Berlin, and Baden-Württemberg. Germany is an attractive country to visit for young people aged between 15 and 34, who contribute to the positive trend in tourism.

A successful trade fair and congress centre

In 2014, for the 11th time in a row, Germany maintained its position as the no. 1 conference and congress centre in Europe. In the international congress centre rankings

≡ LIST

- Biggest airport: **Frankfurt am Main**

- Biggest railway station: **Leipzig**

- Biggest port: **Hamburg**

- Biggest trade fair grounds: **Hanover**

- Biggest spa resort: **Wiesbaden**

- Biggest public festival: **Oktoberfest**

- Biggest amusement park:
  Europa-Park, Rust

An attractive Alpine panorama: the many foreign tourists who visit Bavaria appreciate the idyll

Germany is in second place behind the USA. Every year 2.7 million guests from Europe alone come to trade fairs in Germany, which is regarded as the most important trade fair location. In 2014, a total of 25.6 million international participants attended events in Germany. In particular the "magic cities" of Berlin, Dresden, Düsseldorf, Frankfurt am Main, Hamburg, Hanover, Leipzig, Cologne, Munich, Nuremberg, and Stuttgart are the magnets for foreign guests. First and foremost among them is Berlin, which in 2014 recorded 11.9 million visitors, and some 28.7 million overnights. In terms of absolute figures for overnight stays the city is in third place in Europe after London and Paris.

According to a survey conducted by the German National Tourist Board the top international visitor attractions include classics such as Neuschwanstein Castle and ▶

▶ Cologne Cathedral. The numerous UNESCO World Heritage sites, among them Sanssouci Palace in Potsdam and Classical Weimar, are also popular. In addition, events such as the Oktoberfest in Munich, with around 6.3 million visitors the world's biggest public festival, also attract visitors. A football stadium is also on the list of tourist magnets: the Allianz Arena, a masterpiece by Swiss architects Herzog & de Meuron, and the Bayern Munich home ground.

Like culture, movement in general plays a big role in Germany's appeal. Around 200,000 kilometres long, the network of hiking trails alone offers extremely good conditions and magnificent views, for example on routes through the national parks or against the backdrop of the magnificent Alps. On top of this there are more than 200 well-established long-distance cycle trails covering 70,000 kilometres, for example the Iron Curtain Trail (1,131 kilometres) or the 818-kilometre long German Limes Cycle Route. Those looking for a cheap night's accommodation will find plenty of opportunities, for example in one of the 500 youth hostels, 130 of which are family youth hostels, or on one of the 2,870 campsites.

Feel-good holidays and environmentally friendly travel

Wellness is an important topic in Germany. It includes such unusual features as the river sauna in the Emser Therme thermal complex, as well as the numerous feel-good facilities in spa resorts such as Bad Wörishofen and Bad Oeynhausen, with its Wilhelminian-era architecture. In Germany, there are a total of 253 spa resorts, which use a label recognised by the "Deutscher Heilbäderverband", the German Association of Spa Resorts. The quality of the medical treatment and support also attracts numerous guests to Germany.

Ever more frequently, travellers are not only taking care of their own wellbeing, but are also paying attention to the environment. In Germany, the demand for ecological tourism and sustainable travel is growing. Organic farms offer holiday rooms, there are 104 nature parks and 15 biosphere reserves, in which great importance is attached to sustainable development and biodiversity. In order for everyone to be able to move around easily in Germany countless initiatives ensure that the disabled too can travel without hindrance.

ⓘ INFO

Climate In Germany a warm, moderate rainy climate with westerly winds prevails. Major fluctuations in temperature are rare. There is rainfall throughout the year. Mild winters (2 °C to –6 °C) and not too hot summers (18 °C to 20 °C) are the rule. In 2014, the mean annual temperature reached a record 10.3 °C, which was 2.1 degrees above the long-term average of 8.2 °C for the international reference period 1961 to 1990. 2014 was 0.4 degrees warmer than the previous warmest years 2000 and 2007.
→ dwd.de

⊙ MAP

Travelling within Germany

● The top destinations

The 11 "magic cities" have a market share of around 43 percent of all overnight stays by foreign guests in Germany. Berlin lies clearly ahead of Munich, Frankfurt am Main, and Hamburg. 55 percent of overnights by foreigners are in cities with 100,000 inhabitants.

✈ The most important airports

The three biggest airports in Germany are in Frankfurt am Main with 59.6 million passengers, Munich with 39.7 million, and Düsseldorf with 21.8 million in 2014.

★ The most popular attractions

According to a survey conducted by the German National Tourist Board, in 2014 the three most popular attractions among foreign tourists were Neuschwanstein Castle, the Europa-Park amusement park in Rust, and Cologne Cathedral.

Attractive tourist destinations in the former East Germany

The five federal states that formerly made up East Germany play a major role in tourism. After Reunification, tourism proved to be an opportunity for many regions in eastern Germany to put themselves on a sound economic footing. Areas of countryside such as the Spreewald biosphere reserve, cultural centres with long-standing traditions such as Dresden and Weimar, and Baltic seaside resorts such as Binz on the island of Rügen attract tourists from Germany and abroad.

Since 1993, the number of overnight stays in eastern Germany has more than doubled. With over four million, Mecklenburg-Western Pomerania in the north east is almost on a par with the state of Bavaria in the south when it comes to holiday trips of more than five days' duration. No matter how much one has already seen – as a travel destination Germany still has more to discover, experience, celebrate and marvel. ■

TOPIC
SPORTING CHALLENGES

Germany is a country of sports enthusiasts and indeed a successful sporting nation. In the Olympic Games all-time medals table Germany, with 1,682 medals (as at 2014), places third behind the USA and the Russian Federation. Around 28 million people in Germany are members of one of the more than 91,000 sports clubs. Alongside their sporting duties, the clubs also assume important social and inclusive roles. Particularly as regards youth work and integration they reinforce values such as fair play, team spirit, and tolerance. Given the rising internationalisation of the population, the work done by sports clubs is becoming ever more important with a view to the social integration of migrants. Around 60,700 clubs have members with a migratory background in their teams. Overall it is safe to assume that approximately 1.7 million people with a migratory background are members of a sports club. Nonetheless, the group of people with a migratory background is still under-represented in organised sport.

The German Olympic Sports Confederation's "Integration through Sport" programme believes immigration enriches German sport. One of the areas the programme will be focussing on in its work in the future will be groups which have previously been under-represented in sport, for example girls and women. Together with the "Bundesliga-Stiftung" and the German Football Association, the Federal Government has also launched an integration initiative. This finances sustainable projects for integrating refugees in sport. These include the project "1:0 für ein Willkommen" – 1:0 for a Welcome – which the German national team supports; the project provides financial assistance to around 600 football clubs that help refugees.   ▶

MILESTONES

1954
Germany wins the World Cup for the first time in Switzerland (beating Hungary 3:2 in the final). The "Miracle of Bern" becomes a lasting symbol of post-War Germany.

1972
The Olympic Games in Munich are overshadowed by Israeli athletes being taken hostage and murdered by Palestinian terrorists.

1988
Steffi Graf becomes the first female tennis player to win the Golden Slam, i.e., all four Grand Slam tournaments plus an Olympic Gold medal, in a single calendar year.

Winning the 2014 World Cup in Brazil: one of the many highlights in German sport

2004

Grand Prix racing driver Michael Schumacher wins his seventh world title (from 2000 to 2004 five times in a row) and becomes the most successful Grand Prix driver in history.

2006

With its official motto "A Time To Make Friends", the World Cup be-comes an unforgettable "summer fairy tale" and puts Germany in a highly favourable light abroad.

2014

Having shone throughout the tournament in Brazil, the German football team once again be-comes World Champion (beating Argentina 1:0 in the final). It is Germany's fourth World Cup title since 1954.

▶ **The German Olympic** Sports Confederation is an umbrella organisation for German sport and sees itself as Germany's largest civic group. It promotes top-class and grass-roots sport. More than 20,000 of the 91,000 sports clubs it represents were founded after German Reunification in 1990. Founded in 1900, the German Football Association is also one of the 98 member organisations. The seven million members in 25,000 football clubs represent an all-time high in the Association's history, and it is the world's largest national sports association.

Women's football is one of the fastest growing sports disciplines. The German women's national team has won the World Cup and the European Championships on several occasions. Motivated by the success of players like Steffi Jones, who in 2016 will become the national coach, some 337,300 girls up to the age of 16 are now active members of football clubs.

The Bundesliga, the top-flight league in German football, is the shining light in German sport. Internationally it is regarded as one of the strongest leagues. In the 2014-5 season, the 306 matches played between the 18 Bundesliga teams were watched live in the stadiums by around 13.3 million spectators, an average of 43,530 per game. Bayern Munich is the measure of all things in German club football. In May 2015 the club won the German championship for the 25th time, on top of which it has lifted the German Football Association Cup 17 times, and in 2001 and 2013 was victorious in the Champions League. With more than 251,000 members, it is the club with the most members in the world after Benfica Lisbon.

The German men's team has won the World Cup four times and the European Championships on three occasions, and is the flagship of German football. Having

The J.P. Morgan Corporate Challenge in Frankfurt am Main is the biggest road race of its kind in the world

won the 2014 World Cup in Brazil, Germany heads the FIFA World Rankings. Trained by Joachim Löw, the team is considered to be tactically flexible, and stands for a modern interpretation of the game. The national team squad includes several players with a migratory background, such as Jérôme Boateng, Sami Khedira, and Mesut Özil.

**Sporting recognition and success
in various disciplines**

Alongside football, popular sports are gymnastics, tennis, shooting, athletics, handball and riding. But other sporting events are also highly successful, for example the J. P. Morgan Corporate Challenge in Frankfurt am Main. Raced by over 70,000 participants from 2,780 companies, the corporate charity run is regarded as the biggest event of its kind in the world.

German sport is a success story in many respects. This is thanks in no small measure to the promotion of sport. This way, around 3,800 athletes from almost all Olympic disciplines, traditional non-Olympic sports, as well as disabled and deaf sport are sponsored. Supporting athletes who have disabilities is likewise an important aspect. And here too, having now won a total of 1,492 medals (2014), athletes from Germany have been highly successful at international competitions and the Paralympic Games.

"On the Move – Overcoming Borders" is the motto of the International Sports Promotion

🌐 **GLOBAL**

Anti-Doping Initiatives
With the founding of the World Anti-Doping Agency (WADA) in 1999 and the commitment of all stakeholders to a zero-tolerance policy towards doping, the need arose for a uniform set of rules that applied world-wide. This was implemented for the first time in 2003 with the foundation of the World Anti-Doping Code (WADC). The latest World Anti-Doping Code came into force on 1 January 2015.
→ wada-ama.org

programme of the Federal Foreign Office. It is a firm part of its cultural relations and education activities abroad, and has already supported more than 1,400 short and long-term projects in various sports in over 100 countries. One example is the sport project "Kicken statt kämpfen – Bolzen für Toleranz", which involved 16 female and male football coaches receiving training in kids' and youth football. The idea is for youngsters suffering from the long-term effects of violent conflict to address the idea of fair play through games.

In this and many other ways, German sport is striving to reach levels of excellence as a means of crisis prevention, and understanding between peoples, and as an ambassador for more fairness, tolerance, integration, peaceful competition, and performance. ∎

🖵 PANORAMA
ATTRACTIONS IN BERLIN

Mitte

Friedrichshain-Kreuzberg

Berlin Districts
A. Mitte
B. Friedrichshain-Kreuzberg
C. Pankow
D. Charlottenburg-Wilmersdorf
E. Spandau
F. Steglitz-Zehlendorf
G. Tempelhof-Schöneberg
H. Neukölln
I. Treptow-Köpenick
J. Marzahn-Hellersdorf
K. Lichtenberg
L. Reinickendorf

❶ Kaiser Wilhelm Memorial Church
Off Kurfürstendamm, the landmark of western downtown, an anti-war memorial.

❷ Victory Column
There are 285 steps up to the viewing platform, from where there is a fantastic view of the city.

❸ Reichstag Building
Home of the Deutscher Bundestag, the German parliament. The glass dome is a real magnet for visitors.

3,420,000
inhabitants

11,900,000
tourists

2,399,000
visitors to
Museum Island

175
museums and
collections

❹ Brandenburg Gate
Every Berlin tourist knows
the Brandenburg Gate,
the symbol of German
Reunification.

❺ Potsdamer Platz
The face of modern
Berlin. The complex
was developed after
the fall of the Wall on
an enormous piece of
waste land.

❻ Gendarmenmarkt
One of the most beau-
tiful squares in Europe
boasts no less than
three Classicist-style
monumental structures.

❼ Checkpoint Charlie
The Wall is no longer, but
the former military checkpoint still rekindles memories of the Cold War.

❽ Museum Island
The five major museums
house some of Europe's
finest collections.

❿ East Side Gallery
The elaborately painted remains
of the Wall are nowadays the
world's longest open-air gallery.

**❾ TV Tower on
Alexanderplatz**
Berlin's TV Tower on
the "Alex" can be
seen from afar, and
from the sphere
there is a view of the
entire region.

505,771
visitors to the
Berlin Film Festival

4,400,000
visitors to the zoo

4,650
restaurants

190
bars and discotheques

TOPIC
LEISURELY ENJOYMENT

Since the beginning of the millennium, German wine has seen a veritable renaissance internationally, which has much to do with the term "Riesling miracle" and is to a large extent embodied by a young generation of vintners who focus more on high quality than high profits. The long growing season and comparatively low summer heat ensure German wines are refined and do not have a high alcohol content.

German wines are grown in 13 areas in which, across a gross area of around 102,000 hectares, a large variety of wines typical of each particular region are produced. Given the amount of land used, and a grand total of about 80,000 vineyards, Germany is, compared with other countries, one of the medium-sized wine-producing nations; in 2014 production stood at 9.5 million hectolitres. Organic wine has a market share of between four and five percent. The German wine growing areas are some of the most northerly in the world. Apart from Saxony and Saale-Unstrut they are primarily located in the south and southwest of the country. The three biggest growing areas are Rhinehessen, the Palatinate, and Baden. Almost 140 types of grape are grown, whereby some two dozen are of major significance for the market, primarily the white Riesling and Müller-Thurgau varieties. There is a split of about 65 percent white wine and 35 percent red wine, whereby pinot noir and Dornfelder are the most important varieties of red grape.

Germany is also a beer-loving country. German beer is appreciated primarily on account of what is in some cases a centuries-old brewing tradition practised by small family and monastery breweries. The Beer Purity Law of 1516, the world's oldest food law, applies to all German beers without exception. It states that apart from water, hops, and barley, no other ingredients may be used. Between 5,000 and 6,000 sorts of beer are produced in Germany, most of them are Pilsner beers; overall, however, consumption is falling.

There is no clear picture for eating habits in Germany. On the one hand, many consumers

NUMBER

282

restaurants in Germany, more than ever before, were awarded one, two, or even three Guide Michelin stars in 2015. Eleven restaurants were include in the top 3-star category. Germany thus maintained its position as the European country with the most 3-star establishments after France, the country of gourmets.

→ restaurant.michelin.de

Big-city flair: in Berlin, as well as in other German cities, there is a lively restaurant scene

are becoming increasingly health and fitness-conscious, and are opting for balanced nutritional concepts. On the other, megatrends such as mobility and the ever greater number of different personal lifestyles are clearly influencing eating and drinking habits.

The German restaurant scene is as vibrant as it is diverse – and is one of the best in Europe.

Alongside top-class, fusion cuisine, and chefs increasingly catering to vegetarian and vegan dishes; old vegetable varieties such as parsnip, turnip, and Jerusalem artichoke are enjoying a renaissance. They are the pillars of the current boom in all things healthy, seasonal, regional, and the taste of home regions. A young generation of chefs is reinterpreting classic dishes and spicing them up with global influences. ∎

PICTURE CREDITS

INDEX

IMPRINT

Facts about Germany

Publisher
Frankfurter Societäts-Medien GmbH, Frankfurt am Main, in cooperation with the German Federal Foreign Office, Berlin

Concept and Chief Editors
Peter Hintereder, Janet Schayan
Project coordination
Andreas Fiebiger
Editors
Johannes Göbel, Martin Orth, Dr. Helen Sibum
Authors
Matthias Bischoff, Dr. Eric Chauvistré,
Constanze Kleis, Joachim Wille
Art direction
Martin Gorka
Panorama info graphics
Einhorn Solutions
Production
Kerim Demir, André Herzog

Translations
Dr. Jeremy Gaines

Frankfurter Societäts-Medien GmbH
Frankenallee 71–81
60327 Frankfurt am Main, Germany
Internet: www.fs-medien.de
Email: tatsachen@fs-medien.de

Federal Foreign Office
Department of Culture and Communication
Werderscher Markt 1
10117 Berlin, Germany
Internet: www.auswaertiges-amt.de
Email: 608-R@auswaertiges-amt.de

Printing
Werbedruck GmbH Horst Schreckhase
34286 Spangenberg, Germany
Printed in Germany 2015

Deadline for copy
September 2015
ISBN
978-3-95542-169-4

"Facts about Germany"
is published in the following languages
Arabic, Chinese, Czech, English, Farsi, French, German, Indonesian, Italian, Japanese, Korean, Lithuanian, Polish, Portuguese, Russian, Spanish, Turkish, Ukrainian and Vietnamese

"Facts about Germany" online
www.facts-about-germany.de